Why people are enthusiast latest book, *Hatr*

"From Cain to today's Islamist, from Hitler, and from Martin Luther to the hatred has been a part of the landscape of the human heart. Tragically, my own family has experienced this firsthand as grandparents, aunts, uncles and cousins—35 in all—were murdered in the Nazi death camps. Why? For one reason alone...they were born Jewish. It is an obsession that dwells deep in the souls of men, conceived by Lucifer himself because of his hatred of the Most High, and it has given birth to some of the most heinous evils this world has known. Victor Schlatter captures the depth and nuances of this obsession, explores the 'meat' of the problem, and his insights are truly revealing. This book will speak to both Jew and Gentile. It will guide you to eschew from your heart any remote lingering of anti-Semitism. Most importantly, it will inspire you to be a lover of the Most High and of the people that He has chosen to fulfil His purposes."

Daniel Robitshek, MD, FACP, SFHM, Instructor in Hebraic Studies, Congregation Beth Aliyah, Associate Professor of Medicine, Medical College of Georgia, Rome, Georgia

"With the rise of global, genocidal anti-Semitism around the world, it is crucial that Christians understand the root of this ancient hatred and our biblical responsibility to stand against this growing threat to our Jewish brethren and all Israel. This book is a must read for anyone who wants to understand the root of this hatred and what those of us who love our Jewish brethren and Israel can do to confront it."

Laurie Cardoza-Moore, President of Proclaiming Justice to The Nations and UN Envoy to the Middle East for the World Council of Independent Christian Churches

"Tragically today we are witnessing increasing manifestations of anti-Semitism around the globe at levels that rival the 1930s. In *Hatred of the Jew*, Victor Schlatter tackles this ancient hatred head-on. In this brave exposé, Victor sheds light on the nefarious propagations of this hatred found in the writings of many so-called 'church fathers,' and quite properly correlating anti-Semitism with being anti-God. From Islamic terrorists to intellectual humanists, Victor exposes that the story is always the same, hatred of Abba manifests through hatred of the Jewish people. Thank you, Victor, for having the courage to tell it like it is!"

Rev. Gary Cristofaro, Director of Development, Ezra International

"It has been a few years since my good friend Victor Schlatter published his last book, and his fans will find his current offering worth waiting for. Victor's last book dealt with where Israel's Lost Tribes will be found. His latest work deals with a much more revealed phenomenon: anti-Semitism and anti-Semites.

"Really, these two groups are two sides of the same coin. As the Prophet says, all of us humans are part of the same family, so your choice is to love your brother or otherwise—neutrality is not an option. And so it is with Victor's writings: you can love 'em or hate 'em, but you can't be oblivious because the topics that he describes are coming at us fast and furious!"

Gidon Ariel, Director, Root Source www.root-source.com
and the Holy Land Bible Bee www.HolyLandBibleBee.com
Founder of the Facebook group, "Jews Who Love Christians Who Love Jews (And The Christians Who Love Them)"

"I have finished the inspiring gauntlet of all 11 chapters. Needless to say it was a trip full of revelation and cryptic slices of pure Irish wit! I have taken courses in literary stylistic analysis in which I had to analyse such mountains of literary accomplishment as Sir Herbert Read, T.S.Eliot's voluminous poetry, Johnathan Swift's *Gulliver's Travels*, Jean Paul Sartre and his raving atheism, John Steinbeck's *Grapes of Wrath*, Ayn Rand's *The Fountainhead*, and more—a wide swath of literature enjoyed (and endured in some cases), but none of them could touch Victor in his style of shrinking entire movements, philosophical giants, and religious fallacies to single phrase descriptions. Like poetry, he reduces the essence of meaning, pompous abstractions that try to pass off as truth, but are stripped bare and left skeletal at the side of the road of life's truth, no longer worth regarding at the fountain of spiritual values. In other words, I revel in his writing!"

Merv Watson, founder of Kings Court Ministries,
Catacombs Productions Ltd., Abbotsford, B.C., Canada

Hatred of the Jew

Victor Schlatter

Evergreen PRESS

Mobile, Alabama

ISBN 978-1-58169-576-2
For Worldwide Distribution
Printed in the U.S.A.

Evergreen Press
P.O. Box 191540 • Mobile, AL 36619
800-367-8203

Table of Contents

Dedicated to the Creator and Designer
of His servant-family of Abraham
whom He chose and assigned
to usher in
His Messiah

This book is all about them. . .
and Him.

Foreword

A Collage of Commentary on the Jew Across the Centuries

There were other voices to introduce the exposé of Jew hatred, but what could be better than eight authentic echoes from history? May we hear them out:

Winston S. Churchill:

Some people like the Jews, and some do not.
But no thoughtful man can deny the fact
that they are, beyond any question,
the most formidable and most remarkable race
which has appeared in the world.[1]

Leo Tolstoy:

What is the Jew?
What kind of unique creature is this
whom all the rulers of all the nations of the world
have disgraced and crushed and
expelled and destroyed;
persecuted, burned and drowned,
and who, despite their anger and their fury,
continues to live and to flourish.
What is this Jew
whom they have never succeeded in enticing
with all the enticements in the world,
whose oppressors and persecutors
only suggested that he deny (and disown) his religion...
and cast aside the faithfulness of his ancestors?!
The Jew is the symbol of eternity...
He is the one who for so long had guarded

the prophetic message and transmitted it to all mankind.
A people such as this can never disappear.
The Jew is eternal.
He is the embodiment of eternity.[2]

John F. Kennedy:

Israel was not created in order to disappear—
Israel will endure and flourish.
It is the child of hope and the home of the brave.
It can neither be broken by adversity
nor demoralized by success.
It carries the shield of democracy and
it honors the sword of freedom.[3]

David Ben Gurion:

In Israel, in order to be a realist,
you must believe in miracles.[4]

Johann Wolfgang Von Goethe:

Energy is the basis of everything.
Every Jew, no matter how insignificant,
is engaged in some decisive and immediate pursuit of a goal.
It is the most perpetual people of the earth.[5]

John Adams:

I will insist the Hebrews have [contributed] more
to civilize men than any other nation.
If I was an atheist and believed in blind eternal fate,
I should still believe that fate had ordained the Jews
to be the most essential instrument for civilizing the nations...
They are the most glorious nation that ever inhabited this Earth.
The Romans and their empire
were but a bubble in comparison to the Jew.[6]

Eric Hoffer:

The Jews are a peculiar people:
Things permitted to other nations are forbidden to the Jews.
Other nations drive out thousands, even millions of people,
and there is no refugee problem.
Russia did it. Poland and Czechoslovakia did it.
Turkey threw out a million Greeks and
Algeria a million Frenchmen.
Indonesia threw out heaven knows how many Chinese—
and no one says a word about refugees.
But in the case of Israel,
the displaced Arabs have become eternal refugees.
Everyone insists that Israel must take back every single Arab.
Arnold Toynbee calls the displacement of the Arabs
an atrocity greater than any committed by the Nazis.
Other nations when victorious on the battlefield
dictate peace terms.
But when Israel is victorious it must sue for peace.
Everyone expects the Jews
to be the only real Christians in this world.[7]

Mark Twain:

If statistics are right,
the Jews constitute but one percent of the human race.
It suggests a nebulous dim puff of stardust
lost in the blaze of the Milky Way.
Properly, the Jew ought hardly to be heard of,
but he is heard of,
has always been heard of.
He is as prominent on the planet as any other people,
and his commercial importance
is extravagantly out of proportion

to the smallness of his bulk.
His contributions to the world's list of great names
in literature, science, art, music, finance, medicine,
and abstruse learning
are also way out of proportion
to the weakness of his numbers.
He has made a marvelous fight in this world, in all the ages;
and has done it with his hands tied behind him.
He could be vain of himself, and be excused for it.
The Egyptian, the Babylonian, and the Persian rose,
filled the planet with sound and splendor,
then faded to dream-stuff and passed away;
the Greek and the Roman followed; and made a vast noise,
and they are gone;
other people have sprung up
and held their torch high for a time,
but it burned out,
and they sit in twilight now, or have vanished.
The Jew saw them all,
beat them all,
and is now what he always was,
exhibiting no decadence, no infirmities of age,
no weakening of his parts,
no slowing of his energies,
no dulling of his alert and aggressive mind.
All things are mortal but the Jew;
all other forces pass, but he remains.
What is the secret of his immortality?[8]

Let us uncover more of their secrets, their pain, and their triumph
in this volume!

Preface

It's not strange that the people group who has their finger-prints on 75% of the pharmaceuticals that deck the halls of human healing and has earned the highest percentage of Nobel Prizes per capita globally should be identified on Palestinian television as the "sons of apes and pigs" Why? For the same reason we hear the following in the media in one form or another:

- In the beginning God created heaven and earth and that He created man in his own image—male and female created he them—for the very purpose of same sex marriage (why else?).

- Islam is a religion of peace although Islam did truly cut off heads from their beginning, but that ISIS is not really Islam (so don't worry).

- Freedom of religion holds only for Islamists (is there anyone else around?) and those genocidal Jews are a demonic reincarnation of Hitler from around 1892, approximately 50 years before he died?

- Land-grabbing Jews never set foot—or had a temple—in the land of Abraham, Isaac, and Jacob before the 1880s because the Palestinians, who lived there for 5000 years up to that time, had never noticed any!

At least that's what they tell us on Twitter!

Moreover, Isaiah 5:20 must have been written from Babylon (because Isaiah never heard of Israel according to Hamas), the Almighty's Prophet Isaiah blessed us with:

> *"Woe to those who call evil good*
> *and good evil,*
> *who put darkness for light*
> *and light for darkness,*
> *who put bitter for sweet*
> *and sweet for bitter."*

I hope this exposé of hatred helps someone, somewhere, to make it out of the mire, because at this point in time we need all the help we can get on this George Orwell classic 1984 parody where, "Love is hate and war is peace."

Let's get out of here, and see if we just can't make it home to Jerusalem!

With hope and blessings,

Victor

Binyamina–Giv'at Ada, Israel

Chapter 1

Stereotyping Problem People

For most of humanity, success is a problem—especially if it's a near neighbor and not you! Or maybe it's the friend who got the recognition that you wanted but didn't get. And that's a problem.

So when did the world's oldest hatred get off the blocks? And why? Well, that's what this book is about. And that's a big problem, especially if you're Jewish!

On the one hand, this peek into the past—not to overlook the present—is going to be all about anti-Semitism. There's the big-bucks syndrome, the media manipulators, the blood libels, the cruel jokes, conspiracy cartels, stereotypes, the slander, the subversion—you name it! Of course you'll find a Jew or two in every category—warts and all—from self-hating Jews to traitors of the tribe from Shanghai to Saudi Arabia. But the venom and the perennial scape-goat of the Millennia Award knows no equal!

On the other hand, anti-Semitism doesn't come identified by a prickly little package with a ragged red ribbon. There are plenty of issues and plenty of hang-ups that cause it to happen. There are even a few side issues in relationships that we'll have to consider first.

I was well into my research for this volume when I had an amazing awakening. If we're going to look at anti-Semitism, there will have to be some people we can check out. If there are no people, there can be no anti-Semitism. That's the unpalatable principle that sparked a demented Adolph Hitler throughout his insane "final solution" to get rid of the segment of humanity he despised.

So we're going to have to start with some real people. And then there is a corollary to that. Those people have to have a name, or at the very least, a category. No name, no blame, and no shame! We need identity along with facts and not generalities.

New Frontiers for Ancient Family Fumbles

So it may be helpful if we glance way back to the beginning. Keeping an eye on how it all started keeps us up to date on any and all nuances of nastiness to come. And that would include names that we know—or should know—which will go back as far as Adam and Eve[1] as well as their first two sons, Cain and Abel. And finally, a slithering Lucifer lurking behind that so-called "lollypop tree" should also signal some serious surveillance!

And finally there's one more remarkable revelation that must never be forgotten. *"Thou shalt not"* is hardly the masterpiece of mottoes for the 21st century. Nor was this slogan even an obviously cherished credo back in the fourth millennial BCE. Or for that matter, it didn't even make the cut way back in the deep dark annals of human happenings. The human psyche just doesn't like to be told what to do!

Truth be told, sibling rivalry—aka jealousy—infiltrates four of the earliest famous families of the Ancients in the pristine headwaters of Hebrew heritage. In fact it is featured well across the biblical Genesis account of humanity. Yet it would have hardly been expected to happen within the kinfolk of Abraham—the *exalted father* of many nations—but uncharacteristically, it did!

Our first episode of brothers battling for pole position in a place under the sun is spelled out in Genesis 4:1-11. So with real people with real names plus a tad of insight, let's begin.

"Adam made love to his wife Eve, and she became pregnant and gave birth to Cain. She said, 'With the help of the LORD I have brought forth a man.' Later she gave birth to his brother Abel.

"Now Abel kept flocks, and Cain worked the soil. In the course of time Cain brought some of the fruits of the soil as an offering to the LORD. And Abel also brought an offering—fat portions from some of the firstborn of his flock. The LORD looked with favor on Abel and his offering, but on Cain and his offering he did not look with favor.

"So Cain was very angry, and his face was downcast. Then the LORD said to Cain, 'Why are you angry? Why is your face downcast? If you do what is right, will you not be accepted? But if you do not do what is right, sin is crouching at your door; it desires to have you, but you must rule over it.'

"Now Cain said to his brother Abel, 'Let's go out to the field.' While they were in the field, Cain attacked his brother Abel and killed him. Then the LORD said to Cain, 'Where is your brother Abel?' 'I don't know,' he replied. 'Am I my brother's keeper?' The LORD said, 'What have you done? Listen! Your brother's blood cries out to me from the ground. Now you are under a curse and driven from the ground, which opened its mouth to receive your brother's blood from your hand.' "

This spells out the starting blocks for a good preview into a fledgling form of anti-Semitism—ironically it was a single division in a single family. We start from the ground up. And from there we can move on, as soon as all the pertinent points are in place, and connect the dots with precious little problem.

From Stone Age Siblings
to Adolph's Final Solution

This opening saga of two sons does carry a double insight for me as we begin to follow the flag of anti-Semitism. But we need to begin with a tad of background on where I'm coming from. Most recently it's been a 50-year off and on tenure in the South Pacific with its unique Stone Age transition into modernity in the 1960s.

If you recall, those were the days when Western sanity slipped a bit backwards, except for the South Pacific that effected a great leap forward. And I happened to be there! If you check out our South Pacific Island Ministry website[2] you will learn from *Israel and the Islands* on the main menu that there are at least ten references in the book of Isaiah alone suggesting Messianic praise to the Almighty in the end of days—plus a bit more.

My participation in the Pacific added to my knowledge of and love for the Hebrew Scriptures. It was one more intimacy with the era of the Ancients. In one sense, going back to the beginning, I've been there, done that. I've spent just over five decades in what modern anthropologists link to a fading finale of the Stone Age. The era has no relation to dates decided by later historians but rather to how they actually lived.

They synthesized their own fig leaves by creating skimpy grass skirts for the ladies and loincloths for the men, they made stone axes from sharpened flint and razor-sharp paring knives of split bamboo, and they were in total oblivion to other cultures on far away shores.

Thus I must share this sketch of interfacing with similar circumstances of those first recorded biblical names and recognized families including their on-again, off-again, confrontation with a far-off Creator's sovereign choice of design. Ironically they did know of a High God[3] and the culture was a breath of fresh air from a Hellenistic, humanistic, and Aristotle-shackled society.

Could this give us any hint of the earliest of anti-Semitic roots? Even from some social discontent from deep within the family? We'll be checking it out.

Darwin dug into the deep distant past as well—maybe even deeper. Monkey business or not, he probably did not personally name his subjects because God told Adam to do that,[4] and I doubt Darwin bothered to review the effort. One very serious thing that Charlie did not have, however, was people's names and family records.

Contrariwise, the Stone Age we had entered did have names, and families—and to be honest, a civil problem or two! But this re-emphasizes our bottom line, anti-Semitism will have people, they will have names, and there will be contention!

So what in the world was my formerly Western family of six doing so close to environs of a by-that-time disgraced and down-graded Garden of Eden? Unfortunately, we got there a tad late in time and the cherubim[5] were long gone, but there was much else to interest the researcher!

But talk about a learning laboratory in everything from Anthropology to Psychology and human behavior! I have been awarded that and more! I initially had been a nuclear scientist in my younger years, pouring from test tube to test tube and spinning centrifuges, until one day I saw a tiny ad in a no-nonsense, morals-motivated magazine that ranked costly challenges well above cheap sensation. The simple confronting ad: *"Professionals: do something with your life"* caught my attention. I shortly left the laboratory behind and re-tooled over the next two years with the Wycliffe Bible Translators. My wife and I never looked back!

We eventually ended up in the Highlands of Papua New Guinea, a sort of football shaped island just above Australia with an area approximating the size of California. Attacking one of Papua New Guinea's 830 Stone Age, unanalyzed and unwritten languages, we came out after seventeen years with a professional analysis of an anything-but-primitive Waola language. I discovered our Stone Age linguistic treasure-cache had over 100 endings on every verb, and our 17-year marathon included a translation of the Waola Scriptures that was published by our new nation's own Papua New Guinea Bible Society in 1978.

And the experience itself was for real. Kudos included thousands of transformed tribesmen and women that we definitely will meet again one celestial day, not to mention a more mundane several thousand down-to-earth illiterates who now are able to read the Good Book. And that prize in literacy includes at least one post-Stone Age PhD in Law from James Cook University in Australia!

Yet my own personal prize for having invested some five decades of intermittent interaction with a once Stone Age Culture, was the opportunity to enter into and learn deeply from another bygone age at another treasured time. Most of all, it was the stark recognition that the syndrome of success from my former Western World had been infused with a sick set of dead-end, Hellenistic and humanistic oriented values. Without this awakening, this volume on the vile manifestations of anti-Semitism could never have been conceived and written.

Moreover, an Aristotle-free theological worldview is also a welcomed new breeze of Hebraic culture across other of the Pacific Island nations. The most revealing insight is there's not an iota of anti-Semitism in 99-plus percent of Papua New Guineans. And that feature would also be found well across about a dozen other Bible-oriented South Pacific island nations.

Adding that bit of my own background to the mix of immemorial sibling struggle is more than significant. Plus, I've since met not a few other Cain and Abels in our learning curve who are as real as the originals. Human mores have changed precious little, except perhaps for those cell phones that most of our former tribal types now sport across Papua New Guinea!

New Insight for Ancient Subsistence Farming

But there is that one even more momentous cultural note on the response of our once Stone Age family to the translation of the Holy Writ into their mother tongue. Their most vital verse of Scripture was not a Western driven John 3:16. (God forbid that I minimize the importance of that treasured text by this observation!)

Nevertheless, their most meaningful mentoring motto for a Third World value system was that of Galatians 6:7 (KJV)—*"Do not be deceived, God is not mocked; for whatever a man sows, that he will also reap..."* The latter half of the verse in particular was the tenet of truth that transformed a tribe, the Waola literal translation being: *"...the seed you consistently plant, on growing to maturity, you will harvest it and eat it."*

Sibling Cain and a few more of our case studies yet to come, might have beautifully benefitted from similar timely insights. And that's not to recognize that the bitter fruit of victimizing other seeds of the Creator's design, destroys—not only the defenseless and unwarranted victim—but is an even greater lethal poison rebounding back to the planter himself.

Let's move on to a few more unfortunate family failures.

Other Internecine Brothers Battling the Odds

Does it boggle the mind that four of those most famous households in the opening annals of Scripture actually featured feuding families? Hardly! If we search for dysfunctional family feuds in today's fragmenting future, what else is new? Perhaps the irony is that in the Good Book we might have supposed that it's all about the good guys. Not exactly! That could be the case for those who don't read it much—or those who don't think all that deeply when they do read.

Let's check out a few more case studies of sibling sectarianism.

The next fractured family was hardly different from modern mess-ups—one father but two mamas and two half-brothers—Abraham, Sarah, Hagar, Ishmael and Isaac—all in a cross-cultural bridge of chaos. You possibly may know the story. If not, I suggest you check it out first in Genesis 16—all twelve verses. And then for the "rest of the story" (as the late Paul Harvey used to say), shoot across to Genesis 21:1-21. Review that issue as well, and it will give you a much better grasp on where they—and we—are heading.

Father Abraham had thrown a great party about three years after the birth of the second son, Isaac, his long-awaited and hoped for heritage. But the next thing you knew, teenage Ishmael had seized the moment to verbally abuse toddler Isaac during the otherwise festive occasion—no jealousy here of course! Nevertheless, that family flap sent the slave mother of Ishmael packing back to her native Egypt.

Much earlier, even before her son was born, the pregnant Hagar had fled in a somewhat similar flutter, heading back south across the desert toward her former homeland, when God's angel spoke to her concluding with the ominous prophecy: Genesis 16:12:

> "The angel of the LORD also said to her: 'You are now pregnant and you will give birth to a son. You shall name him Ishmael, for the LORD has heard of your misery. He will be a wild donkey of a man; his hand will be against everyone and everyone's hand against him, and he will live in hostility toward all his brothers.'"

Is anyone who is currently observing the bloodletting in Syria, Iraq, IS, ISIS, ISIL[6] and the surrounding Middle East in 2014—and even long before that—at all surprised?

So obviously there was even more trouble ahead. Much more! Clearly the Most High knew all about these futile facts long before they came to fruition—and He still does! Could the intention of the Maker of Mankind have even been to set up prophetic sign-posts signaling danger well down the road?

The bottom line: There might also be a bit of human dissatis-faction in the way the Almighty unilaterally chooses to do things, both then and now, including the family setting in which He has planted us without even asking our permission! Food for thought: Do we get upset with those people who cast a shadow across our comfort zone that disturb us? Or possibly it's really the unseen Planner who is behind it all? Or perhaps it's both?

Double Trouble

Then there's that next-to-come Hebraic family generational scene—with twins! The following layer of legacy unfolds with an Isaac long grown-to-manhood. Then in the course of time, his wife Rebekah bore him a set of twins. And again as the renowned Paul Harvey was wont to add, there's a bit more to the story!

It's all in Genesis 25:21-26a:

"Isaac prayed to the LORD on behalf of his wife, because she was childless. The LORD answered his prayer, and his wife Rebekah became pregnant. The babies jostled each other within her, and she said, 'Why is this happening to me?' So she went to inquire of the LORD. The LORD said to her, 'Two nations are in your womb, and two peoples from within you will be separated; one people will be stronger than the other, and the older will serve the younger.'

"When the time came for her to give birth, there were twin boys in her womb. The first to come out was red, and his whole body was like a hairy garment; so they named him Esau. After this, his brother came out, with his hand grasping Esau's heel; so he was named Jacob."

May I slip back once more into my Stone Age Learning Laboratory from my linguistic and translation days back in Papua New Guinea? Remember that my PNG friends had no current window whatsoever into Western culture until we arrived on their shores in 1961. But they did have legends of origins unknown, four of which would have walked straight out of the Hebrew Scriptures. Here was one of them:

> "Once upon a time there were two brothers. The older one cooked his sweet potatoes—the PNG staple—and set them out to cool. Traditionally, Western culture mentors us to prefer our entrees hot! The younger brother clandestinely came along and nicked off with his older brother's spuds, who upon the shock of his departed dinner, sets out to kill his junior menace. Understandably, the younger lad got out of there big-time. The end of the tale was that after many, many years when the younger son had long grown to manhood, he eventually returned home from a far distant country, not a little wiser—and we must note— certainly, not a little wealthier!"

Does the story ring a biblical bell? If you don't know the Scriptural parallel in its entirety, you'll be taken aback to check it out again in Genesis 27.

I find that account from the annals of the ancients most fascinating, not to mention the blame game that shackles humankind across millennia, perhaps even more than we might have presumed.

An Entire Family Gets in the Fray

Finally, we discover one more Exhibit A in our tales of anti-Semitic testing. Little Jacob in the above story grows up and has not twins but twelve sons. Unfortunately, Patriarch Jake gets so excited when son number ten comes along—and there were reasons—that he emotionally goes over the top. And everyone knows it—not the least, those nine older brothers! Let's check the record in Genesis 37:2-4:

> *"This is the account of Jacob's family line. Joseph, a young man of seventeen, was tending the flocks with his brothers, the sons of Bilhah and the sons of Zilpah, his father's wives, and he brought their father a bad report about them. Now Israel loved Joseph more than any of his other sons, because he had been born to him in his old age; and he made an ornate robe for him. When his brothers saw that their father loved him more than any of them, they hated him and could not speak a kind word to him."*

Then as the story plays out—young Joseph has a couple of dreams—Gen 37:5-11:

> *"Joseph had a dream, and when he told it to his brothers, they hated him all the more. He said to them. 'Listen to this dream I had: We were binding sheaves of grain out in the field when suddenly my sheaf rose and stood upright, while your sheaves gathered around mine and bowed down to it.' His brothers said to him, 'Do you intend to reign over us? Will you actually rule us?' And they hated him all the more because of his dream and what he had said.*

> *"Then he had another dream, and he told it to his brothers. 'Listen,' he said, 'I had another dream, and this time the sun and moon and eleven stars were bowing down to me.' When he told his father as well as his brothers, his father rebuked him and said, 'What is this dream you had? Will your mother and I and your brothers actually come and bow down to the ground before you?' His brothers were jealous of him, but his father kept the matter in mind."*

Eventually, Jacob one day sent Joseph out to find his brothers tending their sheep as recorded in Genesis 37:17-20:

> "...*So Joseph went after his brothers and found them near Dothan,*[7] *but they saw him in the distance, and before he reached them, they plotted to kill him...'Here comes that dreamer!' they said to each other. 'Come now, let's kill him and throw him into one of these cisterns and say that a ferocious animal devoured him. Then we'll see what comes of his dreams.'"*

Of course, as you know, there's much more to the story of Joseph in the closing chapters of Genesis. The kid whom his brothers hated eventually shot up an unlikely totem pole to become the Prime Minister of Ancient Egypt, and consequently morphed into the means of the entire family's miraculous deliverance from starvation across a devastating seven-year famine.

Thus our probe into the roots of hatred toward the Jew, the world's oldest scapegoat as it were, proceeds! But significantly, these case studies had not at the first involved broad cultures or nations, but simply stark and generally fiery division within single families[9] which were—except for this fourth example—frequently quite small in number. Ironically, as noted previously, they were in fact all representations from the same Hebrew lineage that—it would appear—ultimately spread to the same evil flames of venom, blame, and vitriol across the globe.

It might suggest that the blame game is mere human nature until it becomes obvious that the stereotyped Jew has evolved into the favorite target—dumping ground if you please—across most of humanity. He has become the scapegoat that the world loves to hate!

How and why? It will involve detailed history and may be multi-faceted, but we are heading for realistic insight that makes more sense than mindless happenstance! Moreover, in my down-to-earth "Stone Age classroom" of over five decades, I have learned that of life's five question words of who, when, where, how, and why—why is the granddaddy of them all. Keep that one in mind as we move on into probing full blown anti-Semitism.

So for now, we will further build on our insights into those first four nuclear families as we continue to crack open other subtleties of our probe into Human Spirit 101. As already noted at the beginning of our observations, due to our biblical sources, they have all been Hebrew families and, more significantly, all do happen to hail from a heritage of "chosenness."

Though confident of the reality of what we may see already falling into place, I neither am one to fudge to facts nor to stack the deck. Moreover, the last thing I would want to do is to give opportunity to the biased mindset of those bigots who chose to do so.

So let us continue on into an even wider scope to probe a common denominator of culpability for the world's oldest blame game. And once more I conclude that the Bible is the most credible place to continue checking the records of humanity's hiccups across eons of malevolence, misfortune and pain.

Anti-Semitism doesn't come
in a prickly little package
with a ragged red ribbon.
There are issues–plenty of issues.

Chapter 2

An Expanded Family
in a Wider Wilderness

Up to now we have been delving into four Hebrew nuclear families of biblical renown, all four of which had been riddled with internal squabbles. Unfortunately half of these as a result of the early-on friction have, over the millennia, morphed into irreversible ideologies—Ishmael and Isaac and Jacob and Esau. Cain and Abel ended in a murder of the younger sibling, while two of the four involved a further planned or attempted murder—Jacob by Esau and Joseph by his 9 brothers. That doesn't say much for the odds in this part of the world at this part of the study!

So if the domestic environs were a bit too crowded for harmony, let's see for one more time how these early tribal test cases not so triumphantly toughed it out across wilderness turf as they escaped out of slavery in Egypt to higher plateaus of expectation of better days to come. Here's Exodus 16:2-3:

> *"In the desert the whole community grumbled against Moses and Aaron. The Israelites said to them, 'If only we had died by the LORD's hand in Egypt! There we sat around pots of meat and ate all the food we wanted, but you have brought us out into this desert to starve this entire assembly to death.'"*

And we continue in the same scenario in verses 6-8:

"So Moses and Aaron said to all the Israelites, 'In the evening you will know that it was the LORD who brought you out of Egypt, and in the morning you will see the glory of the LORD, because he has heard your grumbling against him. Who are we that you should grumble against us?'"

Moving ahead to Numbers 11:4 we have much the same complaining:

"The rabble with them began to crave other food, and again the Israelites started wailing and said, 'If only we had meat to eat!'"

One thing is becoming clear as we look for a tad of light at the end of the proverbial tunnel: Those Hebrews—or at least a great many of them—must have been quite ordinary human beings like the rest of humanity, warts and all. We all can nurse a bit of self-pity at times or get grumpy with the ground-rules, can't we?

However, they were not specifically a wretched or cursed race either, as a perverted Adolph Hitler and his current Middle-Eastern protégés with medieval mindsets of anti-Semitic bigotry would have the world believe about those so-called chosen "infidels." Rather it would seem to be that it was the Creator whom the majority of those complainers would actually like to see in the dock! Is there anything else new?

Indeed, the Hebrews-cum-Jews all the way back to the get-go did have their share of problems. Just ask Tevye[1] of *Fiddler on the Roof* renown who reaffirmed that they were the chosen people but wondered why God sometimes couldn't choose someone else."

So just where will that proverbial fly in the ointment land next?

More Doom in the Desert

Next in the biblical queue of desert despair is a candidate named Korah, an overambitious activist from the highly esteemed tribe of Levi, no less. This Korah along with a few of his fans insisted that there must have been an overdose of lackluster leadership as they crossed that inhospitable desert.

He challenged those "self-styled" leaders, Moses and Aaron, that in his mind they were, after all, only an insider clique in the clan, who were not only giving the Hebrews a bad name but also giving all those weary, trudging travelers a tough time to boot.

But could Korah have gotten it right in Numbers 16:1-3?

"Korah son of Izhar, the son of Kohath, the son of Levi, and certain Reubenites—Dathan and Abiram, sons of Eliab, and On son of Peleth—became insolent and rose up against Moses. With them were 250 Israelite men, well-known community leaders who had been appointed members of the council. They came as a group to oppose Moses and Aaron and said to them, 'You have gone too far! The whole community is holy, every one of them, and the LORD is with them. Why then do you set yourselves above the LORD's assembly?'"

Who lobbied in this Moses, this expat from Midian, into top management anyway?

If we read on, Numbers 16:28-35 verifies that the choice was made by the Most High, Himself.

"Then Moses said, 'This is how you will know that the LORD has sent me to do all these things and that it was not my idea: If these men die a natural death and suffer the fate of all mankind, then the LORD has not sent me. But if the LORD brings about something totally new, and the earth opens its mouth and swallows them, with everything that belongs to them, and they go down alive into the realm of the

dead, then you will know that these men have treated the LORD with contempt.'

"As soon as he finished saying all this, the ground under them split apart and the earth opened its mouth and swallowed them and their households, and all those associated with Korah, together with their possessions. They went down alive into the realm of the dead, with everything they owned; the earth closed over them, and they perished and were gone from the community. At their cries, all the Israelites around them fled, shouting, 'The earth is going to swallow us too!' And fire came out from the LORD and consumed the 250 men who were offering the incense."

The fire may have been hot, but the total tale quite chilling! It's pretty clear that in the eyes of the Almighty, the major hiccup was hardly culpability in lackluster leadership that hindered their headway! Nor was it Moses and Aaron who tarnished Father Abraham's respectability with legalistic leadership.

The actual contention, of course, was whether the chain of command should have been with the more democratic bloc of well known community leaders or the more theocratic choice of Moses and Aaron.

Perhaps we might review the incident with those Hellenist experts from Athens. Enter the classic contribution of Greek mentality by Pericles, the highly esteemed Father of Democracy: "There's always a more democratic way to do it!" Yet historically, Pericles was a mere Johnny-come-lately to the earlier rebuttal by Levite Korah: "Moses, you got it all wrong. We're all holy—who do you think you are?"

This kind of thinking of course comes straight out of Aristotle & Co's handbook. Fortunately for Pericles, Athens was not in the Wilderness Journey GPS, and the Wilderness Journey was not exactly via Athens. As a consequence, when the time arrived, Pericles probably had a more standard burial than did protégé Korah!

Mind-bender Pericles[2] may have had some good ideas, notwithstanding, but like forerunner Korah, he may not have collected all his facts in time. I plan to award him my mini-memorial "Churchill Prize," summing up wily Winston's catchy appraisal that "Democracy was the worst form of government there was"—with the wry addendum, "except for all the others."

Nevertheless Pericles himself finally got voted out big time in the 2012 election of Mohammad "Sharia-stained" Morsi in Egypt in 2012. Why do I say that? He had the democratic numbers to support him alright but hardly the confidence of a secular Egypt, and they finally threw him out of office and put him in jail for subversion.

And my own addendum is that democracy was hardly the Ancient of Days' idea either. It has its benefits when the nasties are all out to lunch! But it was a Greek humanistic philosophy from the Aristotle Alpha to the Hellenist Omega!

The democratic principle can certainly be helpful when a community of ideas is pliable enough to agree to disagree, but when it is concocted to amalgamate two or more diametrically opposed philosophies, it's a dead loss in more ways than one. Anyway, Moses kept his marching orders in the desert, regardless of Korah!

Finally before we leave Moses—the most highly cherished Tour Guide Israel ever had—he did have a few other antagonists. Unfortunately, within the last few years—and even hitting new tsunami heights especially since the recent Gaza flood of media manipulation—global anti-Semitism is even higher now than in Adolph's abominable 1938 levels. Even once moderate churches are into disgraceful anti-Israel bias.

Among this burgeoning multitude of Jew-haters, one pseudo-sanctified schism of Presbyterians[3] has joined those raucous cries of the activist University BDS radicals to once and for all economically strangle this "legalistic" Moses-mob for good. Even if all the college campuses across the Western World were to effectively Boycott, Divest and Sanction Moses' floundering flock (aka the Zionists), they could never dent the Israeli economy. But it just rubs salt into the wounds of mindless centuries of sectarian bias and bigotry.

Or perhaps I didn't get the above acronym right, and BDS actually stands for Brainless, Deceived and Stupid, as they broadcast their venom on a bandwagon of all these other so-called intellectuals from institutions of higher (aka: leftist) learning. It's amazing how little humanity has intellectually advanced in all of three millennia!

This might be a good point to question how anyone with functioning grey matter in his head or a grain of gratitude in his soul can face up to historical statistics and ignore reality to denigrate a Jewish culture that has given us the Bible from Above, while here below they garner the highest number of Nobel prizes per capita and produce the highest percentage of pharmaceuticals on the shelves of the globe's medical institutions.

Moreover, this is not to pay notice to all other matters of ingenious benefits of science and compassionate medicine. But instead, callous hatred, hoping to overturn the obvious verdict of superb value and appreciation for what the offspring of Abraham and Moses have contributed to humanity from time immemorial.

Or how could these giants of genius suddenly morph into the vilest vermin on earth, reflecting the most contemptible crowd in the galaxy? Someone hasn't done his homework and is cheating big-time in an attempt to pass his finals!

From the so-called holy books of the most populous medieval-minded religio-political system on earth, their offspring have been taught for generations on end that Jews are the progeny of pigs and monkeys and are destined to be slaughtered. How can this blatant perversion ever get past the pretense of an "even-handed" United Nations that serves all people or so-called political correctness that supposedly represents an elite mentality of the 21st century? And why can the UN be blindly bereft of honesty in these matters and the European Union so callously bigoted as they also "hear no evil" and paint the Jew with a broad brush of brazen bias? Something is obviously seriously wrong! Is it the democratic principle applied to an overpopulation of ludicrous lemmings?

Perhaps it's a maxim I learned for Bible translation decades ago: "No one is as blind as he who does not wish to see; no one as deaf as he who does not wish to hear!"

And speaking of Bible translation, let's get on with a bit more Bible in the next section.

A King Like the Nations

So let's move on from those early wilderness boondocks like Horeb, Sinai, Kadesh and the Arabah and follow the Israelite readjustment from 40 years of a nomadic life style in the desert, to settle into those current boundaries known today as Judea and Samaria. These were the major land divisions that Joshua under Moses' directive—and the authority of God Himself[4]—had divided among the twelve tribes. These comprised the communal districts spread among the tribal allotments to Benjamin, Judah and Ephraim and their brothers. These three were somewhat more central and thus became the heartland of Jacob's inheritance promised by the Almighty to Father Abraham.

And from Sinai on, their designated Levitical leadership was known as Priests or sometimes Judges, and eventually certain of the more prominent Prophets were recognized and revered as God's sovereignly selected ambassadors.

Having considered that much communal background, we move on to the next Hebraic transgression being "political incorrectness" as recorded in 1 Samuel 8:4-7:

"So all the elders of Israel gathered together and came to Samuel at Ramah.[5] They said to him, 'You are old, and your sons do not follow your ways; now appoint a king to lead us, such as all the other nations have.' But when they said, 'Give us a king to lead us,' this displeased Samuel; so he prayed to the LORD. And the LORD told him: 'Listen to all that the people are saying to you; it is not you they have rejected, but they have rejected me as their king.'"

Just as we might have known; but there's more in verses 8-9:

"As they have done from the day I brought them up out of Egypt until this day, forsaking me and serving other gods, so they are doing to you. Now listen to them; but warn them solemnly and let them know what the king who will reign over them will claim as his rights."

Under the Bus with the Prophet Samuel

Empathizing with a now kicked-under-the-bus, Prophet Samuel, is it back to Pericles and those "enlightened" Greek Hellenists, or is it "who cares what the people want"?

Would real kings actually do it better? Like Stalin and Hitler, or Nero and Hadrian, or maybe Putin versus a let-me-change-the-world Barak Obama!

If you don't mind, I'll take the Ancient of Days, thanks!

Centuries later, totally apart from Samuel's untimely rejection, the Prophet Isaiah sums up the same scenario as the self-willed civilization of his day is confronted by his simple analogy of the lowly potter's wheel of Isaiah 29:15-16:

"Woe to those who go to great depths to hide their plans from the LORD, who do their work in darkness and think, 'Who sees us? Who will know?' You turn things upside down, as if the potter were thought to be like the clay! Shall what is formed say

to the one who formed it, 'You did not make me'? Can the pot say to the potter, 'You know nothing'?"

And we connect the narrative again in Isaiah 45:9-15:

"Woe to those who quarrel with their Maker, those who are nothing but potsherds among the potsherds on the ground. Does the clay say to the potter, 'What are you making?' Does your work say, 'The potter has no hands'? Woe to the one who says to a father, 'What have you begotten?' or to a mother, 'What have you brought to birth?' 'This is what the LORD says—the Holy One of Israel, and its Maker.'

"'Concerning things to come, do you question me about my children, or give me orders about the work of my hands? It is I who made the earth and created mankind on it. My own hands stretched out the heavens; I marshaled their starry hosts.' This is what the LORD says...They will bow down before you and plead with you, saying, 'surely God is with you, and there is no other; there is no other god. Truly you are a God who has been hiding Himself, the God and Savior of Israel.'"

So what can we conclude in these two opening chapters? The most primitive seed-bed of anti-Semitism took the form of "more Hebraic" versus "less Hebraic" over conflicts in four key families of earliest biblical record. And as the nuclear family units morphed into larger communal groupings, the sibling styled contention did not disappear but only grew into larger communities, each supporting their side of the issue.

Therefore, if the reader has not yet noticed, the current tsunami of so-called anti-Semitism hardly began with the outsiders but began as a totally internal malady of discontent. There was discontent with local leaders and even a call for a king that was the hallmark of the pagan nations around them. Or was it their Creator's culpability who told them things they neither liked nor really wanted to do? And finally as the cookie of old cryptic consensus crumbles: If you have four Jews, you'll get at least five opinions!

Thus, we're going to have to dig for even deeper roots to get into today's pandemic of anti-Semitism, and we're going to have to have to find some Gentiles. We had thought all along that these outsiders were the really bad guys! Maybe some of them still are?

So let's go looking for some Goyim.[6]

Complaining is
a telltale testimony
that the god you serve
is inadequate.

Chapter 3

The Stranger Within Your Gates

Faithful to what we have found in our previous pages, God's Holy Writ is still the preferred place to go looking for life's clues. And that consequently will never overlook the significance of how the Creator's "chosen vessels of clay" were also intended to correspondingly respect and reach out to the Goyim—the Gentiles aka the nations. Anti-Semitism, of course is a two-way street.

"The stranger that is within your gates" remains a classic *King James Bible* expression. In translation to English, the *New King James* (NKJV) retains this poetic form, while the *New Revised Standard Version* (NRSV) uses the words *alien within your towns*, the *New Living Testament* (NLT) says *foreigner*, and the *English Standard Version* (ESV) calls the outsider a *sojourner*.

Thus, here are a few examples of how the keepers of the gate are supposed to treat the outsider within these word pictures from the book of Deuteronomy:

• In Deuteronomy 5:14, regarding the observance of the Ten Commandments, the NRSV includes the presumed compliance also by *"the resident alien within your towns."*

• In Deuteronomy 14:29 on giving hospitality, the NLT says it should be extended to *"the foreigner living among you."*

• In Deuteronomy 26:13 on sharing the tithe of the harvest, the ESV translates it "I have given it to…the sojourner."

• While in Deuteronomy16:14 at the Feast of Tabernacles, King James and the NKJV uses the familiar: "And you shall rejoice in your feast, you…and the Levite, the stranger…and the fatherless and the widow, who are within your gates."

Whereas the specific words in Hebrew that are translated into the above four English variations may or may not be understood to specifically include the Gentiles—aka nations—neither is there a specific rule why it would not be so. It depends on any and all rabbinic interpretation—remember four Jews, five opinions!

Nevertheless, rather than deciding to open this chapter with a concrete clarity from the text, I deliberately chose to begin the chapter with this example of less certainty of whether the term *stranger* may or may not include the Gentiles.

Why? Because of our following considerations of numerous examples that do show that inclusion of the outsider is bedrock to Judaism; and more than that, because these next instances of bona fide acceptance of the Gentile are so strong and significant that they will deliver the initial "within your gates" discussion from all doubt for any and all relevance of who can or who can't come to the party!

The Mixed Multitude

Perhaps our most unambiguous inclusion is that the "mixed multitude" (Exodus 12:38) on the exit lane out of Egypt, pursuing freedom from Pharaoh, departed as a unit on the night of that first Passover. Circumcision for the males was always a future requirement for Passover participation, but with the haste[1] of departure, it was hardly a time as well for surgical procedures for all foreigners.[2] All parameters from Sinai had not yet been issued; moreover, there were no second-class campers!

Most of the foreigners integrating as the "mixed multitude" were obviously Egyptians, but there could have been other outsiders conscripted into the work force as well.

Some of the ethnically mixed Egyptians were the offspring of Joseph, the sons and daughters of Ephraim and Manasseh whose mother was a full blown Egyptian. A mixed multitude is a mixed multitude! And they became one company on the freedom track.

A bit later, Jethro, the Midianite—Moses' father-in-law—also joined the journey, and even had some good advice for son-in-law Moses in Exodus 18:17-22:

> *"Moses' father-in-law replied, 'What you are doing is not good. You and these people who come to you will only wear yourselves out. The work is too heavy for you; you cannot handle it alone. Listen now to me and I will give you some advice, and may God be with you. You must be the people's representative before God and bring their disputes to Him. Teach them the decrees and laws, and show them the way to live and the duties they are to perform. But select capable men…who fear God, trustworthy men and appoint them as officials…have them serve as judges for the people at all times…'"*

My own paraphrase: "Moshe, my boy, you're working too hard, you'll never make it up that mountain—get some help."

For more mix to the multitude, Moses' wife and two sons, Gershom and Eliezer, clambered into the crowd. She of course was full Midianite and the boys were half, and I dare guess that their now-grown sons would already have each been starting a family.

And to round out the reunion, brother-in-law Hobab shows up in Numbers 10:29-31 and for brothers-in-law—who are not always the best of buddies in a Western culture—Moses gives his Midianite relative the warmest of welcomes, and even implores him to join the march in Numbers 10:32:

"If you come with us, we will share with you whatever good things the Lord gives us."

Now let's pick up the irony of what a mixed multitude is all about—to rub shoulders with the forefathers of the humongous horde of Midianites that later did battle with Gideon in Judges 7 and in later skirmishes as well.

So for Hebrew hospitality, they probably didn't do too badly for putting up with one another for 40 years across intolerable turf. Unfortunately they even likely agreed that manna was not exactly their favorite Trail Mix and were unanimous in their complaints against Moses, Aaron, and the Almighty in that one! Remember what we have already said in Exodus 16:2-8 back in Chapter 2.[3]

Finally at the end of the road—the "Jericho Road" we might note—they made positive contact with the Canaanite Innkeeper, Rahab, who may have been unjustly stereotyped by her job description[4] but regardless of what some folks may have guessed of her occupation, the bottom line is what she did for the Israelites. She not only blessed Abraham's family[5] but she also saved the lives of all of her family, and became one of Israel in Joshua 6:25:

"But Joshua spared Rahab the prostitute with her family and all who belonged to her because she hid the men Joshua had sent as spies to Jericho—and she lives among the Israelites to this day."

Not bad for Israelite warmth and compassion to a Canaanite, and she even got her name a few times in the Good Book for Honorable Mention![6]

The Furnace of Affliction

Having thus far followed the bonding relationships among our Mixed Multitude—as the King James Bible called them—they painfully plodded together for 40 years over unchartered desert.

Evidently they eventually got to know each other a bit! Did you suppose that they might have picked up another specific name that identified this on-again, off-again people-movement, unprecedented in both timing and numbers?

Indeed they did. Perhaps the most common description in English was simply the *congregation,* which ultimately functioned as a unit. The KJV used this term a maximum 333 times; while the new KJV, new RSV, New American Standard (NAS), and the ESV each used congregation roughly 140 times to cover the Wilderness trek. The NIV and other translations also used the translation *community* which came a distant second in usage.

Is this name important? I think so. After all, I doubt they used all that much English—or even Greek—on the Moses March! And therefore the Hebrew word that was used should have been significant to later translations!

Kehila is the more characteristic term for *congregation* in Modern Hebrew, and much like English, also known as community in some settings. Kehila is derived from *khal* used in biblical Hebrew,[7] and as a sometime linguist and translator, this stands out significantly as a cognate depicting the congregation during those days of drudgery dragging through the desert.

Now to the precise point! Ironically what was initially called a congregation in Hebrew was later incorrectly interchanged with the Greek terminology *ecclesia.* That in turn began to be known as *church* in English, which unfortunately fit comfortably with a then increasing distance between themselves and anything Jewish, including the kind of comradeship that had been forged in those wilderness wanderings from long ago. It was anything but what we know today as a church. And it is no secret that a part of that name—hardly all—has been a shameful cauldron of anti-Semitism.

An ecclesia, moreover, harks back to a more politically oriented civil council in Greek Athens, and unfortunately it had nothing whatsoever to do with a collection of newly freed Hebrew slaves departing from Egypt and forming a de facto congregation along with a selection of like-minded, non-Jewish fellow travellers.

The terminology for a church today conjures up imagery of everything from signboards to steeples and the "weekly agenda," which would have shaken Moses and Aaron even a bit more than that abrupt burial of Korah and compatriots!

The Hebrew *kehila* for congregation is more like the original idea. After all, it wasn't an air-conditioned church or a cushy synagogue for that matter. It was people! People! People! And that was woven into one massive wilderness congregation—kehila in Hebrew. Truth be told, it didn't matter what they called it, but the name should reflect who they were and what they did!

And of course, that wasn't easy. A collage of some five different references in Scripture refer to the Almighty's forging the House of Israel—warts and all—into the one people designed for His Kingdom in Isaiah 48:9-10 through that furnace of affliction:

> *"For my own name's sake I delay my wrath; for the sake of my praise I hold it back from you, so as not to destroy you completely. See, I have refined you, though not as silver; I have tested you in the furnace of affliction."*

And let's just include one more of those five biblical references to a purifying furnace of future fulfilment from Deuteronomy 4:20:

> *"But as for you, the LORD took you and brought you out of the iron-smelting furnace, out of Egypt, to be the people of his inheritance, as you now are."*

You know, when it comes right down to it, that also almost sounds like the routine battle of life to maintain a decent morality in the 21st century, not to mention coping with bigoted hatred from people who don't even know you and you don't know them!

The Durability of Desert Discipline

We've already had a past preview of those surfing life in a testing crucible. Way back in my younger years I had a lot of learning earlier on in the laboratory, remember? Maybe at the time my experience was more *with* the test tube than *in* the test tube— aka crucible. However, when you're in the wilderness of testing, you win some and you lose some!

So let's next have a look at a couple of cases of those on the ledge of losing what they knew—or should have known.

Back in Chapter 2, the Prophet Samuel had that disappointment of his life—or was it in spite of his life of long service to the sons of desert survivors? Some of that wrought iron forged in the wilderness got rusty before they knew it. How soon do we forget His rainbows!

"Samuel, we need a king!" Actually by that time disenchantment with the Deity did already cover a half of a millennium since the lessons of Desert 101. On the other hand, when we reflect back to Mt. Sinai, it took only 40 days to go from two designer drafted tablets of stone to a grubby golden calf. Blatant back flips should no longer surprise us—from 40 days to even 40 generations.

So we also can move on to Nehemiah's time following the destruction of Solomon's temple. That would have been after 70 years of added Hebrew exile in Babylon, and the Jews were now heading back home to Jerusalem to rebuild from the former ruins. Nehemiah had been nominated[8] from the world stage to oversee the rebuilding the wall of Jerusalem.

Under his watch, there arose another significant problem of memory loss over lessons learned by the ancestors who dragged on through the desert. Now centuries later, again we encounter another "mixed multitude" of near neighbors to get into the act.

But why join up this time? To escape another evil day? Hardly! This time it was rather for subversion. So when Nehemiah and friends came together to read the bylaws—actually, the Law—a different mixed multitude had to be sorted out—and ushered out! Just to clarify about "mixed multitudes," obviously motives do matter![9] Thus we may happen to find strangers within our gate who may be quite on the wrong side of anti-Semitism—not to mention the alternate side of the Almighty!

Infiltrating the faithful for a tad of the take or a cut of commodities are not exactly the right reasons for boarding the gravy train, and Nehemiah had to take a stand.

This is one example of losers at crashing the party, and we'll look at one more in Acts 8. A seemingly spiritually enthused—but a bit of a shady shaman known as Simon—heard the challenging call from Above but like Humpty Dumpty soon had a great fall. He had seen a few genuine miracles among the new believers and supposed this was a superb way to pick up a few spare shekels. But with a tad of added strong advice from the Apostle Peter, Simon came up with egg on his face in Acts 8:20-22a.

> *"Peter answered: 'May your money perish with you, because you thought you could buy the gift of God with money! You have no part or share in this ministry, because your heart is not right before God. Repent of this wickedness and pray to the Lord in the hope that he may forgive you...'"*

Finally, Simon does get it right in Act 8:24:

> *"Then Simon answered, 'Pray to the Lord for me so that nothing you have said may happen to me.'"*

We include this incident, hoping that the U-turn happened, but add this anecdote because not every stranger at the gate may hold a boarding pass!

There are also the big winners. There was the unforgettable episode when Yeshua met up with the Samaritan woman in John Chapter 4.

Just over a year ago, I had the unique privilege of meeting a couple of Samaritan families having a picnic on top of Mount Elon Moreh. That just happened to be the exact prominent point of Abraham's orientation to the Land of Promise.[10] These folks were from the last remnant of 700 Samaritans alive today. One of them gave me his business card from his company in Tel Aviv, which among other things gave the interesting living proof that the Samaritans of today are a bit upscale than they were a millennium ago when Yeshua met this lady at the well in John 4. You can read the tale for yourself, but in those days, women were Samaritan second class and not supposed to chat with Jewish men.

The larger link with the story was that the Son of Man knew her most intimate details that only a Prophet from God could know, and as a result she also did an about face to get to know the God of the Prophet. The rest of the story is in John 4:39-41:

> *"Many of the Samaritans from that town believed in him because of the woman's testimony, 'He told me everything I ever did.' So when the Samaritans came to him, they urged him to stay with them, and he stayed two days. And because of his words many more became believers."*

The bottom line is that this is the kind of "stranger from within your gates" who was the outsider that knew what she wanted, found it, and shared it.

Finally the classic add-on of all time into the people of Promise was Ruth the Moabitess. If you know the story,[11] Ruth and her Moabite counterpart, Orpah, had married into the family of their distant Hebraic cousins from Bethlehem. After a severe famine in the land, Naomi, her husband Elimelech, and their two sons fled from Israel across the Jordan to Moab in search of food. As a result, the two sons, Mahlon and Chilion, in time married two Moabite girls, Orpah and Ruth.

Eventually Naomi's husband, Elimelech, as well as her two sons died and left behind the grief stricken Naomi and her two daughters-in-law. Finally after the famine in Israel abated, a crushed and broken Naomi decided to return to her beloved Bethlehem and bade her two Moabite daughters-in-law goodbye. Orpah returned home.

Ruth instead gave the memorable response in a book that forever bears her name:

> *"Ruth replied, 'Don't urge me to leave you or to turn back from you. Where you go I will go, and where you stay I will stay. Your people will be my people and your God my God. Where you die I will die, and there I will be buried. May the LORD deal with me, be it ever so severely, if even death separates you and me'"* (Ruth 1:16-17).

Orpah returned to Moab and remarried among her people. Even though there was that ancient kinship to the Moabites through Abraham's nephew Lot, the ensuing decadence of the Moabites elicited the curse recorded in the Law: *"A...Moabite shall not enter the assembly of the Lord; even to the tenth generation."*[12]

Biblical research[13] has it that Orpah remarried to eventually connect into the blood line of the Philistines and entered into the maternal ancestry of God-hating, Jew-despising Goliath.[14] Alternatively, Ruth married one Boaz, another Bethlehemite from the linage of her mother-in-law, Naomi, and as a result unintentionally fell into the bloodline of the promised Messiah through David the shepherd boy cum King of Israel. And we must note, David the slayer of the above-mentioned Goliath.

And reinforcing that declaration of Ruth we have heard above:

> *"Where you go I will go, and where you stay I will stay. Your people will be my people and your God my God..."*

Ruth—you are the kind of Gentile we're looking for as a role model for the "stranger within our gates."

And these days there are many more who are joining the

Ruths—and the Naomis into awakening to what basic Bible is all about. It's not always what we do, but who we become!

I repeat that probing anti-Semitism will be complex. People, people, people and their relationships are complex. We'll move on with much more to cover.

Of life's five question words–
who, when, where, how, and why–
why is the granddaddy
of them all.

Chapter 4

The Wisdom of the "Fathers"

Thus far we've been through family feuds, wilderness moods, and outsiders within your gates. But we will continue to search, sort, and study what are the real roots of venom against the Chosen few? And perhaps *why* could even be most helpful.

Thus far the score is Jews (1), Goyim (1), Out of Office—be back on Monday, (1). So much for the polls—let's find some facts!

Now let's have a peek at some very prestigious people, like those early Church Fathers, and pick up on what they had to offer.

The following mini-bios were all taken from: *The Roots of Christian Anti-Semitism* by Malcolm Hay. Hay's research in turn is found in: http://www.yashanet.com/library/fathers.htm

Ignatius, Bishop of Antioch

First let's have a look at Ignatius, Bishop of Antioch, who presided from 98 to 117 AD. In his epistle to the Magnesians, he writes:

> "For if we are still practicing Judaism, we admit that we have not received God's favor...it is wrong to talk about Jesus Christ and live like Jews. For Christianity did not believe in Judaism, but Judaism in Christianity."

Now he said much more than that in what I dubbed as a mini-bio, but this is enough for our purposes, and for which I can evaluate as: Strike One, Ignatius!

Not sure where you got that insight, but it was certainly not in the same Bible that I translated for the Waola Tribe in Papua New Guinea, carefully checked by the Wycliffe Bible Translators and published by the earlier British and Foreign Bible Society.

The Jesus you refer to was a Jew and lived like the Jews of His time. But He did challenge a skewed rabbinic interpretation of the Mosaic Torah[1] by the so-so hierarchy of his day, For example, he cornered his critics who tried to play the "Moses card" on him with John 5:45-47:

> *"But do not think I will accuse you before the Father. Your accuser is Moses, on whom your hopes are set. If you believed Moses, you would believe me, for he wrote about me. But since you do not believe what he wrote, how are you going to believe what I say?"*

And another comeback to his antagonists re their charge of his breaking of the Sabbath: *"Is it better to kill or heal on the Sabbath?"*[2]

Or their lack of knowledge re Spirit-led leeway: *"...have you not read that King David ate the Holy Bread from the temple which was only for the priests to eat?"* (Luke 6:3-4)[3]

Sorry, Ignatius—we suggest you brush up on your Bible knowledge as well as your fumbling with "isms"!

Yeshua declared very clearly that He did not come to get rid of the Law and the Prophets[4] but to fulfill them. A couple of other good renditions of fulfill are to accomplish their purpose in *The New Living Translation* and to complete them in both the *Message Bible* and the *J.B. Phillips* translation.

Justin Martyr

Then there was Justin Martyr, who served the Movement from 138 to 161AD. In a dialogue with one Trypho,[5] Martyr said:

> "We too would observe your circumcision of the flesh, your Sabbath days, and in a word, all your festivals, if we were not aware of the reason why they were imposed upon you, namely because of your sins and the hardness of heart. The custom of circumcising the flesh, handed down from Abraham, was given to you as a distinguishing mark, to set you off from other nations and from us Christians."

Again his mini-bio says much more than that. But once more it is enough for this biblical umpire to call: Strike two Justin! Above all, that's hardly what the Good Book says about the three major festivals of Passover (Pesach), Pentecost (Shavuot) and Feast of Tabernacles (Succot). These are what the Father calls His appointed times for annually meeting with His people. And these days, these very feasts are being kept by a mushrooming number of Bible oriented, no-nonsense Christians.

Better check your other facts as well, including it seems you are suggesting that the pain of anti-Semitism suffered by the Jewish people as being a penalty from obeying God? I don't think you actually meant to say it that way, but maybe you are unwittingly getting closer to what we are looking for in this book?

Origen of Alexandria

Origen of Alexandria (185-254 A.D.) was an ecclesiastical writer and teacher who contributed to the early formation of Christian doctrines. His mini-bio from Malcolm Hay's *The Roots of Christian Anti-Semitism* includes the following perversion:

"We may thus assert in utter confidence that the Jews will not return to their earlier situation, for they have committed the most abominable of crimes, in forming this conspiracy against the Saviour of the human race…hence the city where Jesus suffered was necessarily destroyed, the Jewish nation was driven from its country, and another people was called by God to the blessed election."

Well, well, well. A Christian teacher from Alexandria obviously missed out on most of the Good Book from Isaiah on through Malachi, aka the Hebrew Prophets. The Jews will not return to their earlier situation? Please Origen, your name could hint you may only be at the bare beginning of study. What happened to the rest of the story?

Isaiah 49:8-25 is one of several summaries of the unswerving Old Testament theme that Isaiah entitles The Restoration of Israel along with the following Scriptures:

Beginning with Isaiah 11:12-13:

"He will raise a banner for the nations and gather the exiles of Israel; he will assemble the scattered people of Judah from the four quarters of the earth. Ephraim's jealousy will vanish, and Judah's enemies will be destroyed; Ephraim will not be jealous of Judah, nor Judah hostile toward Ephraim."

Isaiah 49:6 says: *"It is too small a thing for you to be my servant to restore the tribes of Jacob and bring back those of Israel I have kept. I will also make you a light for the Gentiles that my salvation may reach to the ends of the earth."*

Isaiah 49:12: (re Israel's exiles) *"See, they will come from afar—some from the north, some from the west, some from the region of Aswan."*

Isaiah 49:23: (To Israel) *"Kings will be your foster fathers, and their queens your nursing mothers. They will bow down before you with their faces to the ground; they will lick the dust at your feet. Then you will know that I am the LORD; those who hope in me will not be disappointed."*

Jeremiah 31:35-37: (The Promise) *"This is what the LORD says, he who appoints the sun to shine by day, who decrees the moon and stars to shine by night, who stirs up the sea so that its waves roar—the LORD Almighty is his name: 'Only if these decrees vanish from my sight,' declares the LORD, 'will Israel ever cease being a nation before me.' This is what the LORD says: 'Only if the heavens above can be measured and the foundations of the earth below be searched out will I reject all the descendants of Israel because of all they have done...'"*

And finally in Amos 9:11-15 (To a scattered Israel) *"'In that day I will restore David's fallen house—I will repair its broken wall and restore its ruins—and will rebuild it as it used to be...' 'The days are coming,' declares the Lord, 'when...I will bring my people Israel back from exile. They will rebuild the ruined cities and live in them...I will plant Israel in their own land, never again to be uprooted from the land I have given them,' says the LORD your God."*

Then Hosea picks up the classic allegory of the jealous husband (God) forgiving and remarrying His wayward and unfaithful wife (Israel) in Hosea 14:1-3b, and sums up the symbolic story:

"Return, Israel, to the LORD your God. Your sins have been your downfall! Take words with you and return to the LORD. Say to him: 'Forgive all our sins and receive us graciously, that we may offer the fruit of our lips...We will never again say 'Our gods' to what our own hands have made, for in you the fatherless find compassion.'"

And one outstanding final prophetic voice of an Israel forgiven and restored in the end of days is Zechariah's. The prophet fills in the fate of the end of days in Zechariah 12:1-3:

> *"The LORD, who stretches out the heavens, who lays the foundation of the earth, and who forms the human spirit within a person, declares: 'I am going to make Jerusalem a cup that sends all the surrounding peoples reeling. Judah will be besieged as well as Jerusalem. On that day, when all the nations of the earth are gathered against her, I will make Jerusalem an immovable rock for all the nations. All who try to move it will injure themselves.'"*

Then we see Zechariah's prophetic finale in 14:2-4:

> *"I will gather all the nations to Jerusalem to fight against it…half of the city will go into exile, but the rest of the people will not be taken from the city…Then the LORD will go out and fight against those nations, as he fights on a day of battle. On that day his feet will stand on the Mount of Olives, east of Jerusalem, and the Mount of Olives will be split in two from east to west…"*

He winds it up in verses 16-17.

> *"Then the survivors from all the nations that have attacked Jerusalem will go up year after year to worship the King, the LORD Almighty, and to celebrate the Festival of Tabernacles. If any of the peoples of the earth do not go up to Jerusalem to worship the King, the LORD Almighty, they will have no rain."*

And for my own finale for those less-than-focused "Fathers": just in case any of you my readers, would happen to bump into Mr. Origen before I do, let him know that in contrast to his pessimistic prediction on the Jews never returning to their former state, there seems to be a multitude of Jews—according to Zechariah's prophecy above—who are currently making their way back to Jerusalem, much in context with a suggested preparation for the New Edition!

Or should anyone else chance to contact Justin Martyr en route to hopefully better days, let him know that those burdensome Jewish festivals—including Tabernacles—are alive and well, and our real Father hasn't announced any modifications just yet.

Moreover, if somewhere along the line we learn that JM has had a change of heart, remind him to bring an umbrella for just after the feast. Quite in line with Zechariah 14:17 above, right after Tabernacles always begins Israel's rainy season!

John Chrysostom—One of the "Greatest"

Finally, there was John Chrysostom (344-407 A.D.) – One of the "greatest" of church fathers; known as "the golden mouthed" missionary preacher, famous for his sermons and addresses.

Unfortunately, look what he said in a bit of his mini-bio about Abba's Chosen Servants:

"The synagogue is worse than a brothel...it is the den of scoundrels and the repair of wild beasts...the temple of demons devoted to idolatrous cults...and the cavern of devils. It is a criminal assembly of Jews...a place of meeting for the assassins of Christ...the refuge of devils, a gulf and a abyss of perdition...As for me, I hate the synagogue...I hate the Jews for the same reason."

Thus, we see that it is just getting worse as we go through this list of so-called Fathers of the faith who were forerunners of what became known as "the church" aka *ecclesia* in Greek. Indeed with heroes like that, who needs Constantine?

Yet Constantine did show up and made his contribution for better or worse. Moreover, some of the Reformation's eventual re-definers of righteousness[6] get even more decadent with their anti-Semitic vitriol, but we'll check out a few more of them later.

If some have tagged John Chrysostom as the "greatest" from what we have seen thus far I am wondering, the greatest for what? Probably the Ayatollahs of Iran could have used him in their seminaries, or perhaps one or two of the UK media outlets might have relished his rhetoric for blast-Israel broadcasts!

Or in the current Gaza fact-fabrication facilities, Chrysostom would have gone well. I know that there would have been openings for literary contributors to Abbas' Fables or Grim's[7] Fairy Tales for Terrorist Tots[8] in these days of vitriolic hatred of the Jew across the Middle East as well as even unprecedented odium throughout Europe!

Back in Australia—and most likely in the UK—when our Queen Elisabeth is rebuffed, the classic journalistic rejoinder is: "the Queen was not amused."

We can readily use that turn of phrase right now. Having just heard the rhetoric that the politically correct of yesteryear were once taught that "decent people don't talk that way," and also having just left behind those formidable four of the "Fathers" who badmouthed the "beloved" of our One and Only Father, none of us are amused!

But is "beloved" really the best terminology at this point? It definitely is! It behooves us to bounce back to the Good Book: "*...but concerning the election they* [the Jews] *are beloved for the sake of the fathers* [the Hebrew patriarchs]."[9]

And if we need reinforcement with another "witness" how about back to Jeremiah 31?

> "*The Lord appeared to us, saying: 'I have loved you with an everlasting love.'*"[10]

Chapter 5

The Gaza Conflict and Anti-Semitism

Sorry, but I get not a little sarcastic, needless to say, with the poisoned pens from those four so-called sanctified Fathers, all the way to the current depraved perversion of truth and deception out of the Gaza in our day. The most pathetic participants in the encore are those who can't read Arabic, who can't think for themselves, and lap up the political deception like popcorn at the proverbial party!

Then, of course, there are those around the globe who despise Jews and devour the repulsive rhetoric to bolster their own bigotry.

My Palestinian Media Watch files approach 500 damning reports—mostly Hamas TV—monitored by PMW Director Itamar Marcus, an honorable and upright personal friend of mine. PMW translates the blatant and preposterous TV claims from Arabic into English so the rest of the world can fathom the fabrication. Unfortunately the rest of the world does not want to know! Such is the Media's deceptive parallel of Gaza's political war, and the West has been swallowing it like Jonah's whale.

The encounter in Gaza with the added violence of war was not yet in the mill as I was mulling over the format for my treatise on anti-Semitism. Nevertheless, the Gaza intrusion fits hand in glove with any and all menacing hatred of the Jew, so we must address it.

43

We'll touch on it now and we'll also follow up on it later in Chapter 8. Could this too have been in the divine plan?

We were here in Israel for the entire time and monitored the monstrous Hamas deceit and cover-up. We could experience first-hand the terrorism freely provided by the bias of Big Media throughout the firing of some 3000 Hamas rockets upon civilian targets—including a few in our own direction. Yet the globe's bigotry in their anti-Jewish sentiment is beyond belief!

Now most casual anti-Semites won't admit to that, but there are really no other options. Read the blurbs on the Church Fathers again, and if that's not enough, download their accompanying URLs. These so-called Papas had already destined the Jew to the pit of hell. Sadly their studies had somehow never included Chapters 9, 10 and 11 of the Book of Romans!

Plus, a somewhat bitter pill for Christians is when so many of our God-fearing Jewish family fail to see that the vile invective of those infamous Fathers is hardly what the entirety of the church is all about today. Indeed for some, yes, but certainly not all!

What is labeled as the church is anything but monolithic. There is a faithful core of non-Jews that are certainly far more pro-Israel than any secular Jew around. And could there also be a bit of scattered Ephraim at large and aching for home? And there are those Christians that are pro-Israel to a point, but sadly confused by bad doctrines of Hellenist hiccups as we shall note in Chapter 7.

Of course, Satan's subtle but never-satisfied sleight of hand that churns the cauldron reminds one of Solomon's bit of wisdom in Ecclesiastes 1:7: *"All the rivers run into the sea, yet the sea is not full..."* There will always be more twisted truth to come!

Simultaneously, the Gaza war is an ongoing cultural war. It has nothing to do with land, oil, money, real estate, or what is right or what is wrong. It has everything to do with Middle East mentality of who has the right to live or who has the destiny to die. Thus, it is not only a cultural war; it's a religious war, but that's the last thing the kings of the earth want to admit. They have no answer. Fortunately, the Good Book does.

But of course, anti-Semitism has similar parameters. As above, it's not about land, oil, or money, notwithstanding there are ludicrous bigots who maintain that the Jews have all the big bucks. That one-eyed line, of course, reeks with jealousy and greed, but it still determines whether the Jew is worthy of life or death. It's sheer hatred.

The planet—or even heaven for that matter—is deemed not to be large enough for both Islamic and Judeo-Christian ideologies! Thus it's a spiritual problem, and lurking behind it all, is the Ishmael-Esau cum Amalek mindset.

Due to the virulent Hamas propaganda from rigged and censored photography, intensely monitored and highly restricted international journalism, and brain-dead social media, Hamas has now succeeded in fomenting a global hatred of Israel to a higher level than it was in 1938. As noted back in Chapter 2 that was the year Adolph Hitler began his final solution in an orchestrated genocide of world Jewry.

It gets crystal clear from where Hitler, Hamas, Hezbollah, and a hierarchy of Hebrew-Haters got their own first nibble from the Tree of Knowledge of Good and Evil.[1] Yet to come, there will be a bit more insight into the anti-Semitic manipulation of actual facts, bringing the full Gaza debacle into even more clarity in Chapter 8.

So for now, let's pause a moment. Granted that anti-Semitism, which has its roots imbedded into much of the Church, is bad enough, but before we empty the whole truckload of sewage all in one back alley, there are other smelly tankers yet on the road. As we finish this latest insight into anti-Semitism, there are still a few other tunnels burrowed under a sort of global-Gaza that first need flushing out.

The Hellenist Highway to Handle Hebrews

Long before Rome, the Greeks had found a new corridor for conquest. They didn't want to merely massacre most all Jews, because it would only curtail a more humanistic line of human development. The Jew is brilliant. Athens could have used them! They just wanted to change the way the Jew thinks from monotheism to polytheism, but it won't work! Remember the Maccabees.[2]

Thus, the Greek Hellenists didn't win their biggest battles with the sword. It was with the mind. And ideas—good or bad—are always around to fight again another day. This has massive significance as we move from the pre-Constantine Church Fathers on through Rome.

In short, from Genesis on, the God-fearing Hebrews—later known as Jews—were always at odds with pagan, polytheistic Kings who lusted for power and supremacy. When Messianic Judaism—aka Christianity—surfaced, that added a second threat to the sovereignty of the Kings of the earth, to which they must crush in persecution.

Then in 325AD a crafty, calculating Emperor Constantine jumped into the ring to put the church part of monotheism into his hip pocket. In a quote worth remembering from my 2009 book: *Nineveh: A Parody of the Present,* we have: "With wine and wafer in hand, Constantine joined the church."[3] In reality, he took it over. And that left the God-oriented Jews alone in the line of fire. Interesting! How much has this to do with the ever mutating saga of anti-Semitism?

Back in much earlier times, after the death of Alexander the Great in 322 BCE, the vast Greek empire splintered into four lesser entities.[4] After considerable jockeying for leadership and land-scrambling over the next 125 years, the Seleucids eventually gained control over the land of Israel, and in 176 BCE Antiochus IV ultimately inherited the throne over Judea. As noted above, the pagan Greeks were less than impressed with monotheism, nor were the Jews themselves amused by the desecration of their Temple and the corresponding flouting of their Torah.

Fast forward: The Judean Maccabees miraculously whipped the Greeks in 167 BCE and sent them packing, but as alluded to above, Hellenism had already been born. Even though Aristotle had passed away almost two centuries earlier, his worldview lived on after the Maccabean victory to fight again in yet another day.

At the time of this writing, Israel is now locked in a bitter battle with Hamas aka idiomatic Amalek. But as we noted a few pages back, the conflict is not over oil, hegemony, resources, or boundaries. It's over a virulent hatred that would not be won until every Jew is dead. This is in the Bible! God knew human hearts before we did. Exodus 17:16 tells it just like it is:

"He [God] *said, 'They have raised their fist against the LORD's throne, so now the LORD will be at war with Amalek generation after generation'."*

King Solomon recorded a similar observation again in the book of Ecclesiastes 1:9: *"What has been will be again, what has been done will be done again; there is nothing new under the sun."* Western World leaders can't seem to get their heads around these ancient principles because the ancients were not framed in post- Aristotle Hellenistic thinking. Hebraic thinkers should generally catch it, but let me make a point. I said *Hebraic* and not necessarily *Judaic*. Remember today we have four Jews and five opinions?

The principle—whether on the right track or the wrong—is what we might call Middle Eastern mentality. It's embedded in the Quran as well as other of Islam's holy books. In Israel's current conflict with Hamas in Gaza, Israelis reluctantly jest about "mowing the lawn" in Gaza. Because unless Israel disarms Hamas once and for all, the depleted Hamas rocket arsenal and sidelined political misinformation will ultimately grow back and the "grass" will have to again be "mowed" in another day. And that's less than inspiring but it will probably have to happen!

That mindset of Amalek noted in Exodus 17:16 will never change. It can't. For an individual it could, but as a faction it can't. It's locked into history.[5]

> "*You* [Hagar] *are now pregnant and will give birth to a son. You shall name him Ishmael...he will be a wild donkey of a man; his hand will be against everyone and everyone's hand against him and he will live in hostility toward all his brothers*" (Gen. 16:11-12).

And this has everything to do with the historical hiccup that had meanwhile surfaced in Rome, including not a few of the Protestant splinters, Orthodox Jews, Christian Zionists, and above all, anti-Semitism. Let's follow it through.

But before we leave Constantine too far behind—in the same above-cited book[6] covering those five prominent nations across biblical tenure, how long they lasted, and what they did to finally propagate their demise, I dedicated one chapter in part to Emperor Constantine's unique U-turn that summarizes how a Christian-defying Rome could do an about face to head up the novel, new world religion almost overnight. The section entitled "Constantine's Crafty Curriculum" is less than three pages—much too long to insert here—nevertheless too helpful to ignore altogether.

Thus, it would be worthwhile for your review at this point. Many of my readers would already have the book, but it's also available on Amazon or from Evergreen Press, but one way or another, check it out.

Aristotle's Long Shadow Across the Western World

Therefore, having now covered one of Rome's key "founders" of Christianity, let us move on to the next outgrowth of our famous newly formed family.

As we leave Constantine behind, it is certainly not on my agenda to critique the rest of Rome's pros and cons of faith, practice and performance. My track for this volume is one issue and one issue only—anti-Semitism to which I hope to adhere. Whereas, I don't recall the fine print that any of the popes came anywhere near to approaching the malicious invective mouthed by those so-called Fathers, I leave any papal contribution for others to pursue. That's hardly to say it was all a clear slate, but it is to say, that the liability of their leadership is not what any so-called birthday of anti-Semitism is about. It's not who said what, but rather the legacy it left.

However, as we head for Rome, there remain three scenarios subject to survey: Which of the admirers of Aristotle weaseled their way into Rome's pipeline to bring humanistic sentiments into Judeo-Christian theology in general, and Rome's initial approval of Aristotle in particular?

We'll look at the oldest first—that is the influence Aristotle himself, and his parade of partner philosophers who harnessed the Brave New World[7] with what became known as Hellenism. Hellenism is simply the Greek culture fashioned by the philosophy of ancient Greece. In spite of his departure in 322 BCE, Aristotle's worldview in general and his Hellenistic legacy in specific were alive and well in post-Constantine Rome. And his teachings were more than influential.

Here's a truncated blog on the much-magnified philosopher who ended up largely transforming the Middle Ages into what we know as the Western culture today. Perhaps it was inevitable, but how good really was it?

Aristotle[8]
"By far the most important group to us as Protestants in our consideration here is Aristotelianism. The philosophy of Aristotle became so important in the Middle Ages that

it dominated almost all of the medieval universities. It provided not only the forms for the expression of theological and religious truth but also the basis for all scientific study in every field. If a man didn't know Aristotle, he was considered an ignoramus...It was in such universities dominated by Aristotle that young Martin Luther received his education..."

That bit of insight from the end-noted essay on Aristotelianism, fairly well sums up our first "scenario subject to survey" above. It is the influence of Aristotle and Hellenism on the Western World, particularly the shift from Hebraic thinking to Western theology. This essay spares me the struggle of trying to make sure I'm not slinging some self-fabricated slander. Pandora's box is wide open!

That which follows next are four of the most programmed protégées of subtle Hellenistic humanism as a counter culture to biblical, Hebraic bedrock. It seeped in slowly, believe me.

Martin Luther is already mentioned above, but before we get to his specifics, we will consider two of his Aristotle-influenced predecessors among the Catholic clergy.

Saint Augustine surfaced shortly after Constantine in the 4th and 5th Centuries. A short excerpt of his background and political theory includes:[9]

St. Augustine

"Augustine was a major early church theologian and in addition to that a philosopher who contributed vastly to the consolidation and development of early Christianity. All three major Christian denominations: Eastern Orthodoxy, Catholicism and Protestantism venerate him as a saint and follow much of the ideas he developed in his abundant writings. A prolific writer St. Augustine left a voluminous literary heritage which covered not only questions of faith but also questions of pure philosophic nature – his treatment of time (Confessions, XI) being a pivotal example. However, in most instances it is impossible to separate his philosophy from his theology and a careful reader should always bear that in mind. Unlike St. Thomas Aquinas who was a great admirer of Aristotle, St Augustine was more influenced by Neo-Platonic thought. He tried to bind some of the ancient Greco-roman philosophy through Plato and Cicero with the Christian teaching. Furthermore, he put a special emphasis on human free will and divine grace and the importance of the single individual with respect to God which in turn paved the way to early modern thought in the theology of Luther and Calvin. Yet ultimately his pessimism about the capacity of human reason to bring about progress due to the sinfulness of man after the Fall, clearly distinguishes him from the main optimistic tenor of later Enlightenment thinkers...We know a lot about St Augustine's biography because he left a detailed record of his life in his Confessions."

That might be a tad heavy; however, Augustine's entire background can be reviewed in the endnote. Four major points above, however, are worthy of emphasis:

1) Augustine was influential on all major Christian denominations;

2) It was impossible to separate his philosophy from his theology;
3) Aristotle was an influence, but other of the Hellenists were more so; and

4) Augustine himself was a mighty influence on both Luther and Calvin.

This is significant. My major focus of this whole chapter is to follow the dots from Greek Hellenism to Western culture[10] in general and theology in particular. Moreover this is hardly the end of the trail—only the beginning. Keep tuned in. There'll be more fine print in Chapter 7.

Next on the list is that other influential Catholic clergyman, 13th Century St. Thomas Aquinas. And from what we should have seen in the above reports, he was a man who certainly was mightily mesmerized by Aristotle—the acclaimed King of Medieval University philosophical status.

Ironically in our excerpt below from St. Thomas' extensive bi-ography,[11] it says almost zero about Aristotle, yet it says enough. Others above have been over the top on extolling the king of Hellenism's influence on St. Thomas which seems to be our major authority.

St. Thomas Aquinas
St. Thomas Aquinas is also known for writing commentaries examining the principles of natural philosophy espoused in Aristotle's writings: *On the Heavens, Meteorology, On Generation and Corruption, On the Soul, Nicomachean Ethics and Metaphysics*, among others.

It was the writings of Aristotle that influenced St. Thomas' own writings, and once again the pen may prove mightier than the sword, never mind that when it's on paper it could even lengthen itself a few centuries longer!

Or Aristotle's influence spilling over into the 21st century could be summarized with the kid who defined faith as: "Believing what you know ain't so!" We'll have a lot more specifics on Western cultural mindset in pages to come, especially in Chapter 7.

Déjà Vu—History Will Judge Them and How!

Next we'll have to evaluate the overall contribution of those two high profile offshoots of the Reformation who would have had to alter their own personal definition of righteousness, in order to exempt themselves from their denigration of Jews. The first one will be to follow up on how motivated Martin Luther was bent upon blessing Abraham's flock. It seems he wasn't!

Martin Luther

Perhaps the most often quoted essay by Martin Luther was "On The Jews and Their Lies," which he penned in 1543.[12]

> "What then shall we Christians do with this damned, rejected race of Jews? Since they live among us and we know about their lying and blasphemy and cursing, we can not tolerate them if we do not wish to share in their lies, curses, and blasphemy. In this way we cannot quench the inextinguishable fire of divine rage nor convert the Jews. We must prayerfully and reverentially practice a merciful severity. Perhaps we may save a few from the fire and flames [of hell]. We must not seek vengeance. They are surely being punished a thousand times more than we might wish them. Let me give you my honest advice. First, their synagogues should be set on fire, and whatever does not burn up should be covered or spread over with dirt so that no one may ever be able to see a cinder or stone of it. And this ought to be done for the honor of God."

Ouch! And this particular tirade turns even worse with the ten following paragraphs of much more of the same. In a bit of back-pedalling—if it's even decent for me to make excuses—it has been concluded from other writings of Luther that, in the earlier days of his break with Rome, he expressed a much deeper sympathy and compassion for the Jewish people. Then in later years, he did a complete about-face, reversing his former sensitivity with the above vitriolic venom.

Now that's a bit strange, as I think most of us who take eternity seriously would prefer to end our ledger of tongue-lashing in personal relationships the other way around—a bit more mellowed as the milestones mount and Judgment Day approaches. But that's Martin Luther's track record! And there's bit more for follow-up on Luther's legacy in the endnote.[13]

Sorry to say, identical inflammatory rhetoric or worse is currently coming out of Iran, most of the Middle East, and even Europe, in bitter anti-Semitism against the Jew, while the archives on the Third Reich indicated that Adolph Hitler had been notably influenced by those hostile rants of Martin Luther. And this was Rome's theological repairman for the Protestants?

On the other hand, to their credit, large numbers of Luther's liturgical followers today distance themselves from their founder's evil remarks about the Chosen Seed of Abraham. Sadly, other churches of the same era by haughty self-delusion, claim that in the course of history the Almighty decided to dump the Jews for more manageable milestones of theology—like liberal Protestants perhaps?

Regrettably, the anti-Semites don't even bother to review or consider any other reality. They just maintain that it was God who changed His tune—but they of course didn't! Biblical scholars identify the back-flip as Replacement Theology. But Scripture asks of Israel's own backsliding: *"Has a nation changed its gods, which are not gods? But My people have changed their Glory for what does not profit."*[14]

Leaving Luther, the other Reformationist's critique was whether John Calvin had anything nicer to say about Jews than the infamous "Father" Chrysostom did! Obviously he didn't!

John Calvin

Here's John Calvin in: *A Response to Questions and Objections of a Certain Jew.*[15]

"Their [the Jews] rotten and unbending stiffneckedness deserves that they be oppressed unendingly and without measure or end and that they die in their misery without the pity of anyone."

Thus John Calvin had joined the anti-Semitic chorus of abusive epithets against Jews whom they mostly had never met. From Church Father Ignatius to Protestant Reformationists, John Calvin and Martin Luther, there would be mountains more invective to be quoted. There are volumes more written publicizing the quotes of John Calvin[16] who, like Luther, was credited with fanning the flames of anti-Semitism and support of Adolph Hitler across the Third Reich. Appeal was even made by defense attorneys quoting the theological teachings of this Protestant pair in defense of those war criminals later tried and hung at the Nuremberg Trials in October 1946.

But there is already more than enough stain of anti-Semitic garbage smeared across these pages. We don't need more obscene arrogance.

Tragically, lip service to the Spiritual Teacher of these less-than-exemplary 16th Century so-called "role-models" of the emerging Church did leave some positive advice to the true believers:

"Do not judge or you too will be judged. For in the same way you judge others, you will be judged, and with the measure you use, it will be measured to you" (Mt 7:1-2).

Perhaps after fifteen centuries, they took less notice of the above advice, because the one who gave it was—after all—a Jew, and in the Church's new roles of prominence for some of them, Jews didn't count for much anymore!

We're getting to be a bit closer to comprehending the complexity of anti-Semitism.

Chapter 6

Fresh Air from a Pristine Papua New Guinea Worldview

After that bluster from the anti-Semitic badmouthing across Chapters 4 and 5, it's time for some fresh air! As I reported in Chapter 1, I had been facing a new frontier following my earlier-on nuclear science scenario going back into the 1950s. By 1962 I had now begun to break down the PNG language of the Waola Tribe from its original millennia-old spoken form and then transcribe it into its never-before written form, assigning a phonetic alphabet. If that sounds over the moon, also recall that Waola has over 100 endings on every verb, including five tenses.

My point in this is, that's no big deal. Do you know what the starkest revelation of all was? It wasn't my petty performance. I merely had to following linguistic rules that can be learned from textbooks easily enough. The biggie was that the Creator of this whole scenario could have had 20 tenses in His expression of the eternal had He wanted it. But He's so fine-tuned that He has only one tense in His eternal expression of Creation across the galaxies—no beginning and no ending! It's called NOW!

In the English Bible—and I've discovered that this parallels most other languages—Genesis 1:1 starts out *"In the beginning, God..."* Now the reason that English uses "beginning" is because there is a translator's choice to express the Hebrew term *bereshit*." You can translate it as: "In the beginning" or you could say "At the first." Sounds pretty much the same but it's not quite! There is a significant twist.[1]

As we shall see shortly, Hellenistic thinking has a Linear A to B worldview, from a beginning to an ending. That just happens to be the way Aristotle and friends saw the universe.

By contrast, the Hebraic language—including the understanding across the Hebrew Scriptures along with that of the Sages—operates in the comprehension that there is no beginning and there is no ending. That just happens to be the way the Sages also saw eternity—*ha olam* in Hebrew. Life moves in an ever ascending spiral forever upward and ever edging inward toward the Source.

If that sounds a bit crazy, it's only because we're not quite as clever as the Creator is—for sure Darwin wasn't! You just have to concentrate on it for a tad in some quiet corner of a world that has already gone crazy. The Great Designer should be around there somewhere as well to whisper back through His Spirit. This is called thinking outside the box. Most authors have to do that on occasion. It even helps us with finding the right word!

For instance, has the Messiah come yet? If you ask an Orthodox Jew—not yet. If you ask a Goyim (Gentile) Christian—yes, but He'll be back. They both have a point of accuracy.

But when following through with Scripture—if you can appreciate what was just said about the concept of an eternity with no beginning and no end—it means Messiah has been involved since Creation and He'll still be involved at the ingathering of Israel. He was kicked under the bus at one point—actually at many points by many people—but He's back and still with us.

From Exodus 12 through Joshua 4, it is presumed that He is the one who led the Children of Israel through the Wilderness according to Exodus 14:19:

"Then the angel of God, who had been travelling in front of Israel's army, withdrew and went behind them. The pillar of cloud also moved from in front and stood behind them."

He was also referred to as the Rock[2] some 30 times on the trek from Egypt to Jericho; and this Angel of God or Angel of the Lord was so named interchangeably with the Rock about 30 more times in the Hebrew Scriptures.

But make no mistake. This was not some routinely assigned messenger cum angel[3] even if he had a name like Michael or Gabriel. It was the Angel of God or the Angel of the Lord and he carries a special function all through the Holy Writ. Look at the fine print!

Throughout Scripture there are references to God's right arm or right hand. In Numbers 11:23 the Almighty speaks to Moses: *"The Lord answered Moses, 'Is the Lord's arm too short? Now you will see whether or not what I say will come true for you.'"* And in Isaiah 48:13: *"My own hand laid the foundations of the earth, and my right hand spread out the heavens..."*

And Psalms are replete with His reference to His "right hand servant" as in Psalm 80:15: *"The root your right hand has planted, the son you have raised up for yourself."* And in Psalm 110:1 and 5: *"Sit at my right hand until I make your enemies a footstool for your feet."* And: *"The Lord is at your right hand... He will judge the nations..."* And there are dozens more.

Then He also met Joshua just outside of Jericho, and in the book of Daniel—though unidentified as the Angel of the Lord—He joined Shadrach, Meshach and Abednego in the flames of the furnace, and He also showed up as a mystery-man to many, being identified only by the name of Melchizedek,[4] who out of nowhere brought bread and wine to Abraham—frequently known as *Kiddush* in Hebrew or *Communion* in the Gentile world—and certainly there is a good bit of speculation that this particular episode would have been the Messiah out of season as well!

Thus, if by this time you suppose I'm a hopeless heretic, I'll tell you why! You must be thinking more like a Greek than you think like a Hebrew. If you lust for learning more like Aristotle than you ponder His Presence like Moses, so do a lot of other fine folks, but that's why the globe is so full of uncertainty, insecurity, the wrong value system, political correctness, political fantasies like climate change,[5] pansy leadership, and today's intellectual idiocy in general. But there's still hope.

Get Ready for a Deep Breath

We were looking for a breath of fresh air as we begin this chapter. Here's one for starters. As a former nuclear scientist one day I made this ludicrous leap over the moon and landed in Papua New Guinea. Our Papua New Guinea tourist catch-cry is "Like anywhere you've never been." We learned their language, walked their trails, and ate their food. And we learned their lore and lessons. For 50 years it has been an incredible Stone Age learning lab. The Highlanders in particular had never known of life beyond their shores.

Young anthropologists surfaced to write fabulous fables about my new near neighbors to glean fabulous funds from elite universities and prestigious magazines like the *New Yorker* who didn't have a clue what Papua New Guinea accuracy was all about. Who could disprove their ingenious tales? And which by the way includes those blow-you-away documentaries—with Stone Age dress and dances but English sub-titles for sure!

I wouldn't want to suggest that some of this ingenuous information or high-priced photography might not have some treasured insights. After all I do have some far out facts myself. But I do also have not a few names and addresses for follow up if honest accountability asks for it.

On the other hand, in many cases after we had been there for decades, these super anthropology sharpies would come with their cameras and notebooks and after just a few months, they would have PNG by the tail with a downhill pull. For one of the best examples, we had been advised by those three-month miracle analysts that our Highlands inhabitants had themselves trekked to these unlikely shores some 60,000 years ago. Sounds like a bit far out—maybe Mars?

Then some two decades ago when I was talking with one of our neighbors from the Hela Tribe adjacent to our Waola Tribe from the west, we got onto the subject of ancestry and he volunteered information that their ancestor was one Avram Pamu[6] with vital corresponding clues that he was indeed the same Avram/Abram[7] that we can read about in Chapter 12 of Genesis. I had no clue, however, on Pamu until a colleague spied it in the Encyclopaedia Babylonia. But in Babylonia it wasn't Pamu, it was Ramu—a slip of tongue or was it a bit of ear-wax over some four millennia? But the plot thickens. Abram in Hebrew[8] comes from *ab* for father and *ram* for exalted or "exalted father." And Avram Ramu means the "exalted, exalted Father"—the really big guy!

So there's some fresh air, wouldn't you say?

As a one-time scientist, I like to see secrets unlocked and mysteries solved. That's for starters. The word for father in our Waola language is *ab* while with our Hela friends to the west of us, it's *abba*, which is identical to current Hebrew used in Jerusalem. Moreover we have not a few other items related to the Hebrew culture and Scriptures, the flow-on dialect of Avram Ramu. So all of that is a gentle breeze.

I also like to see cheats get caught whether its scientific fudging from four millennia to 60 millennia, or the kid with his hand in the cookie jar, or especially the Most High's hand on the climate control throttle instead of Al Gore and the politicians.

But what does this have to do with anti-Semitism? All along we're getting closer to a universal dissatisfaction as to how the Potter shapes the clay.

A Real Prize from the Pristine Bush

So now let me tell you about Paul Ibagisao, a student from the University of Papua New Guinea.

I met Paul's papa long before he ever tried on a pair of shoes or owned a pair of western shorts. He was sharp; he was personable and became a fast friend in our new homeland in those early days of language learning. The senior Ibagisao became one of the early believers in those boondocks of PNG with a definite new lease on life.

I'm not sure to what degree all of that influenced young Paul, but it certainly must have done a bit genetically for him. There are bedrock biblical promises to parents who tread on a higher plane. But now Paul himself is an upper level thinker in his own right.

Not so long ago we got an email from this young man whose father at one stage had never seen a telephone, a radio, or even an automobile for that matter. To keep out pigs and trespassers, his father had to split out fence posts for his subsistence garden with a stone axe.

But it was a new day. Now a next generation, Paul Ibagisao, was a student and sending emails from the University of PNG which was anything but his Stone Age Pony Express heritage. Young Paul, the thinker, relayed his stark discovery: "Now I have it figured out. We came from God and we're going back to God."

I don't know what this will do to you, my readers, but because I have seen this ancient culture creep online step by step, stone by stone, it blew me away.

This is hardly Hellenistic heresy, but a genuine academic rebuttal of Aristotelian cosmic insight. Though he's a University level student, I'm sure he's never heard of Aristotle or hadn't seen any of those cultural detours that we have been dealing with in the previous chapter—and will deal with even in more detail in chapters to come.

What Paul Ibagisao emailed me was on-the-line Hebrew

thinking. He certainly didn't learn it from his father, nor from me, nor hardly from the University of PNG. It was insight from an even higher level of deduction in an Aristotle free zone.

As I noted previously, Hellenists think in a Linear A to B worldview from beginning to end. But as we have just considered, Hebraic thought has neither a beginning nor an end, ever spiralling upward toward the Divine Designer Himself.

And this might even have much more to do directly or indirectly with the origins of anti-Semitism. The Western World has a good bit to yet unlearn!

A Chosen What?—and a Chosen Why?

In our Rogue's Gallery of Ridicule, we researched in Chapters 4 and 5 about a Sovereign selection of Chosen Servants. It took me a while to sort out what all this Chosenness thing signified. After not a few decades to think this one through, the Chosen People are anything but selected saints—that sounds a bit too much like a Roman recruitment even before we begin. No way! And it's anything but a pretty pansy patch just off your front patio.

This has been a tad hard for the church to swallow—not to mention the world at large—what really does *chosen* mean? Looks like the church as well as the rest of the world will just have to get used to it!

It's been the hardest headache of all for the Jew himself to handle. Sure, it kind of feels good to know that Someone in High Places knows your name, but the minute you step out the front door, how do those folks across the street feel about it? Again we might check up with Tevye.[9]

But look, why were they chosen? What were they chosen for? They were selected out of a good cross-section of humanity. In general, they were reasonably blessed with brains, along with warts and all, so they could be responsible for the Assignment. But they also had bodies with appetites like all the rest of us—again with all the struggles of humanity—so they could be held to accountability. That's a bit different from a knee-jerk concept of goody-goody chosenness.

And what was the Assignment? To enlist a people, a family, an Army of Servants if you will—once more warts and all, to bring in—usher in—the world's Messiah. Did they do it? Once again, you'll get two answers depending on whether you ask a Jew or Gentile. So forgetting the tense bit, let's change that to: Is it on their agenda? The answer is yes, either way.

Therefore, we should re-internalize what Chosen People means. That will never change the bigots; if they are going to be bigots, they're going to be bigots. And it's not really an ethnic problem either; it's a self-image problem. Boys will be boys and bigots will be bigots, and insecure wannabees will be insecure wannabees.

So I suggest we get off this "chosen patsie" concept. The better understanding is "Chosen Servants," which doesn't contradict the Good Book one iota. They are Chosen Foot-Soldiers if you will. Moreover, if we check out the mixed multitude along with not a few others in our previous Chapter 3 or even in Romans 11 in the Good Book, the enlistment office is still open.

Again Tevye might have an answer by now! It gets a bit dicey at times and on the eternal mental jostle of whether the Messiah has already come or not, as we've already discussed near the beginning of this Chapter.

I learned much of this as a post-rocket scientist doing post-graduate studies in that same University on the back side of the mountain where Moses got his degree at Burning Bush Institute of Information aka BBII.

Just to check up a bit on whether you're still on track— do the above insights seem to be edging us any closer to the real root of anti-Semitism?

The Credibility of This Man Named Moses

Who was this Moses fellow anyway?

Some of us have weird and wonderful beginnings. I was a scientist before I turned Bible translator plus a few other things! But Moses got a bit earlier head start. He was a ship captain before he was a tour guide—and a few other things!

I think you've probably heard the story.[10] Old Pharaoh was killing all male Jewish children the moment they were born—so the Hamas in Gaza had really no new ideas—hating Jews is recognized as the world's oldest hatred.

Back to the story, his Jewish mama kind of wanted to keep her cute little guy; so to spare his life, she wove a basket of papyrus, waterproofed it with pitch, and to hide him from the king, sent him sailing securely among the reeds at the edge of the formidable Nile—the youngest sea captain on record! But he eventually grew up.

He got into a hassle with Pharaoh and for his life had to run away into exile in the boondocks of Midian and married a Midianite. (There's a lot more and you'll do well to follow it up.)

But for now, let's pick up a bit of the biblical account:

"Now Moses was tending the flock of Jethro his father-in-law...and came to Horeb, the mountain of God. There the angel of the Lord appeared to him in flames of fire from within a bush. Moses saw that though the bush was on fire it did not burn up. So Moses thought, 'I will go over and see this strange sight—why the bush does not burn up.'...God called to him from within the bush, 'Moses, Moses!' And Moses said, 'Here I am.'...God said, 'I am the God of your father, the God of Abraham, the God of Isaac and the God of Jacob.' At this, Moses hid his face, because he was afraid to look at God" (Exodus 3:1-6 excerpts).

His bio was more bizarre than most. He began in a basket, he escaped an assassination attempt by Pharaoh, he hid out herding sheep, and he encountered the Almighty in a pyrotechnic bush that didn't know when to quit. Was this for real?

For those of us who have a pretty good idea of what was going on here, this incident at the burning bush was no more and no less than one more pre-Messianic appearance of the renowned Angel of the Lord we considered few pages earlier.

One of the first questions that may arise—especially a knee-jerk question of the anti-Semites themselves—is how do we know this to be true? On the one hand, except for the phenomenon of divine faith, we don't. On the other hand, this very impressive human monument to miracles named Moses has had a very long tenure of both respectability and reliability[11] to Jew and Gentile alike, including most all of Einstein's kinfolk! This Moses of biblical renown has been credited with recording the divine dictation of the Torah, the first five books of the Bible that are bedrock to multi-millions of Judeo-Christian devotees.

Now you'll have to be a little bit up on literary genius yourself to appreciate this, but if anyone can enlighten me how this biblical and scholarly tapestry of truth—names, places, statistics, co-ordination of facts, and the cross-consistency of data—can be done by one man without a super-colossal computer of the optimum jillionth generation, let me know of your own research capabilities and we'll do a cross-check on both your parameters of credibility and mine! I have seen some pretty goose-bumpy miracles from over 50 years on the backside of the Mountain in Papua New Guinea to 27 visits to the Promised Land. And by now I know that vast chasm between Real and Rigged!

One personal evaluation I have made is that I have chosen to write all my books in the land of the Bible. Why? I write much more than books, but no where on earth have I found a source of inspiration as in these environs of the geographical inheritance promised to Abraham, Isaac, and Jacob. But is this mere subjectivity? You know what? If it works, I need it! I'll buy the concept! Many of us have come to know well that still small voice[12] from another realm. Moreover, inspiration itself is undeniable, and those who hear it know it unmistakably!

Certainly, subjectivity is always suspect in the human psyche, however, I don't know how many people I've met—religious or otherwise—who acknowledge recognizing much that same phenomenon here in Israel. This is my 27th visit to the land of the Book and that Presence is ever evident. Lift your eyes heavenward or roll them backward—take it or leave it. Along with others who know what I know, I'll take it!

So as we head into the next chapter, as monumental as our hero Moses was, there are still bigots who would deny him, debase him, and discard him. Why? Was it because of his Boss? Well see shortly.

The Creator is so fine tuned that
He has only one tense in His eternal
expression across the galaxies.
It's called NOW!

Chapter 7

Things Not Yet Seen—
Before Constantine

So far we've looked at anti-Semitism in a Hellenized Jerusalem, a Christianized Rome, and a modified Reformation. Which was better—which was worse? It seems that the jury is still out, and you well yet may be tapped for jury duty!

So next we're going to look at a westernized Aristotle, or is it a Hellenized west? Or is there much of a difference?

It doesn't happen to everyone, and it doesn't happen every day; and it doesn't happen in the most opportune time frames that one can step out of his own culture and into another for long enough periods of time to beneficially comprehend the difference. But that may only be a bare beginning. It may take a few more years—or even decades—to fully discern the difference and measure who or what made it, including how and why?

And so it was, after our privilege of investing decades of experience in a Third World culture and eventually we realized that the ancients still possessed something that our own culture had long lost. Some call it "going Troppo."[1] Not quite. Maybe that's a knee-jerk cop-out in denying the value systems of where you had come from and from what you are now able to see!

67

In Papua New Guinea, it was the comparison of a culturally pristine Third World in contrast with a self-centered, humanistic, hedonistic and greed ordered West. The Papua New Guinea we came to appreciate on the one hand was hardly perfection, but it was Aristotle free.

We brought them the Bible—the record of a Creator God's relationship with His creation. No big switch there from any other mission endeavours across centuries. But the real shift was whether it was a Hellenist-humanist ordered culture that was interpreting the Scriptures they were now hearing, seeing, and reading, or whether it was a Hebraic mindset that was measuring the new message they had encountered.

And that was the mighty watershed!

Way back they initially had a worldview that included a heaven-inhabited Sovereign versus earth-bound demons. Hellenism said there were no demons, which would have given PNG one less problem—their main problem actually—that they had to cope with. Unfortunately denial never got anyone over the bar either then or now.

In my involuntary openness, I told them that if they would but have confidence in the God we had come to tell them about, He would take care of those demons. (These were departed ancestral spirits—that impacted their daily lives.) They did and He did!

Ironically they had a tribal name for the one they considered to be their high sovereign: Yegi Gilt, Isi Hobao Sao.[2] The Waola tribe ultimately experienced wave after wave of revival. In actual practice for sure, we still can find a few sinners around, but 50 years on, the tribe in general is 95% Christian oriented—maybe higher.

Now to hark back to Paul Harvey's format once again, here's the rest of the story: After a number of massive revivals by 1988, my wife and I had the privilege of fulfilling a lifelong dream. Doubling with another teaching invitation in Europe, on our return to the South Pacific we had the chance to break our trip in

Jordan and stop over for three weeks in Israel. We experienced the soul of a nation!

Then back to PNG, we of course had personal stories to share that had made our own Bibles spring to life. But it was even more so among our Waola family. They had assumed that only when they died, would they then get to see places like Jerusalem, Jericho and Bethlehem.[3] Not quite. It was now a whole new ball game for Papua New Guinea.

But it wasn't only for our now transformed Waola tribe. Out of widespread interest, across the 1990s I began leading PNG tours to Jerusalem which had included new enthusiasts from all across the some 830 tribes nationwide. Christianized Papua New Guinea became a joint Hebraic oriented Papua New Guinea—all in one!

One can now drive some 700 kilometers from the city of Lae on the easternmost coast to Lake Kapiago well across the Highlands, and on occasion one will see a small Israeli flag on a fence post. Driving a bit further he might see a Jerusalem purchased Menorah on a church door. It's a new day! And I dare say, there is not an iota of anti-Semitism in PNG or in any and all of our near Island neighbors for that matter.

That will therefore declare volumes about what an Aristotle-free Third World nation means, resulting in that same nation being now mesmerized by a biblical Israel.

An Unlikely Visitor and an Even Less Likely Response

One further anecdote worth mention was in 2009 when Isaac, our secular Jewish travel agent from Australia was overwhelmingly curious about what was going on in our heavily booming program in Papua New Guinea including those hundreds now heading off to Jerusalem. This was not only the tours that I had been organizing, but others were spontaneously getting into the act as well.

Far more for the phenomenon than for the business, Isaac took several days off his holiday time to come up to PNG to investigate the new mood. He was literally mobbed—like a Rock Star! Being Jewish, it was the first time in his life that he had ever been in a Christian church, but it was anything from what he might have imagined. There were no crosses, steeples, or stained glass windows—no glass in the windows at all for that matter!

The two pastors and a guitarist would be seated across a long bench in the front of the local materials building while the congregation all sat on the ground conveniently covered with interwoven bamboo plaited matting. Isaac was compelled, however, to sit on that prominent front bench facing the congregation along with the pastors. And they even insisted that he—a secular Jew—share a testimony!

He told them about the first time he met me somewhere in the mid 1980s. Of course there was some singing and some teaching, but this is mostly to report of Isaac's new mountain-top experience and his newly found friends.

The following Monday morning, another piqued congregation from a village about two km away—piqued because they hadn't gotten to host the prestigious visitor—came trudging over the mountain to our home with string-net bags chockfull of vegetables for a social mumu⁴ the following day. They emptied them at Isaac's feet. Semi-apologetically they said, "We know you are not a Christian, but we are of the same family and just want to honor you. After all, who comes way back here to visit us?" An overwhelmed Isaac didn't know whether to laugh or cry!

On his departure he confided to us, "I have travelled the world and have met people who accepted me *even though* I was a Jew, but never in my life have I had people who loved me *because* I was a Jew!"

Compare that one with the vitriolic Jew-hatred that exploded globally after the current Gaza debacle⁵ where the Jew, suffering some 3000 unprovoked rockets onto her civilian soil, was deceitfully inundated by hate-propaganda on social media to inconceivably curse the victim for the crime.

So much for a bigoted Western World and the fresh air of a Hellenist-free PNG society! I began to ponder on what it was that makes such a difference, particularly in the Christian context of my own Bible background. A good share of the fury most certainly must be the subtle anti-Semitic influences of Hellenist-Greek culturalisms into a matrix of short-sighted theological training across the Western world.

No, it's not a twisting of any New Testament teaching or even a bias of translation of various terms or linguistic constructions. We use the same source texts in PNG that they use in the West.

So the translations are okay. It's rather the cultural assumptions swept along with that text. For example, Aristotle ruled out demons and any spirit influence whatsoever, but PNG lived and breathed within this reality, as well as this one-time scientist who himself could now unmistakably recognize demonic presence. The once Stone-agers knew their enemy. Not a bad bit of advice for the politicians of our day.

On a More Private Path

Speaking of science, I have a bit of history to share. I've never attended a Bible training institution, which gives me a totally different understanding of and insight into Western theology. With my degree being in math and science from a Big Ten University in Midwest America, my secular work experience was in Nuclear Energy at the Washington State, Hanford Site of the Manhattan Project, where the first-ever humanly designed production in commercial quantities of a new element named plutonium took its place on the Periodic Table of the Elements. I supervised a laboratory of technicians who monitored water, soil, vegetation, and air samples from the environment of the Hanford Site for the safety of man and beast in the surrounding 586 square miles.

With the foresight of the Father—the only father I ever knew—I had been reading the Bible from a little kid on. And my natural scientific bent was hardly to suggest God's culpability with the Good Book but to prove Him right. Thus in the next five decades or so, I have done just that and then some. As I got a bit older, it became abundantly clear that the novel insights were hardly only for me but for one and all who want to get it right. Today I am an author and analyst of the ancient prophecies that foretold of a day flowing strategically into a decadent humanity that would forget God.

Nevertheless, I did do some biblical graduate training, first in translation techniques from the Wycliffe Bible Translators as well as the British Foreign Bible Society. And translation of the Scriptures was itself a major study programme to say the least!

My biggest boost in theology was my tongue-in-cheek Burning Bush Information Institute[6] on the backside of the mountain in PNG, which I first mentioned in the previous chapter. Nevertheless, the pristine mountains I called home in PNG were not unlike Midian where Moses got his marching orders. Look, I didn't see the Angel of the Lord. He probably was on another assignment by the time I got there, but I sure enough heard and picked up on his message!

And in keeping up with my own insistence to the two or three witness principle,[7] Moses and I were hardly the only lone rangers who made similar inner-soul experiments in isolated backwaters!

There was also this notable fellow named Saul of Tarsus who was friend and colleague at the top levels in Hebraic Orthodoxy in Acts 22:3:

> *"I am a Jew, born in Tarsus of Cilicia, but brought up in this city. I studied under Gamaliel and was thoroughly trained in the law of our ancestors. I was just as zealous for God as any of you are today."*

And not only did he have top training in Orthodoxy, he did a similar independent study in the deserts of Arabia. Let's check that out in Galatians 1:17:

"I did not go up to Jerusalem to see those who were apostles before I was, but I went into Arabia. Later I returned to Damascus."

And by the way, if anyone that thinks that Saul cum Paul was anti-Semitic—he doesn't know Saul of Tarsus. Unfortunately those who thought they knew Saul cum Paul could perhaps have a bit of latent bias themselves. Reversing one's errors upon others is common hiccup in the human psyche!

Am I comparing myself with Moses and Saul, these monuments of the Message? No way! I'm just telling you I was on the same kind of an outside-the-box study program. It's really not all that unusual. Or am I some sort of a nut case? If peanuts qualify in the "mixed nuts" category—possibly I am one! But I'm just ordinary peanuts, not over the top in show business!

One verse from my guiding principle of low profile is explained in Psalm 84:10: *"…I would rather be a doorkeeper in the house of my God than dwell in the tents of the wicked."*

Some time ago in the 90s there was a prophecy given over me, "Don't go with the high flyers" I took it to be from the Most High and I tried to keep on that course. Time and again I was tempted but duly declined to initiate a major independent ministry or personal following.

Our contribution to PNG these days is largely finished, and now from a quieter corner, I write books under South Pacific Island Ministries, and I also put out Israel Awareness Bulletins on my website.

Though they are not exclusively about Israel, I note world events in the flow of prophecy, connecting what is happening in conjunction with what several of the Hebrew prophets said was going to happen. I try to hit on the significance of lesser-known prophecies and not exactly on what the higher profile pundits have run and rerun over the last century or so.

Leaks in the Hellenist Pipeline of Western "Progress"

Did I imply that all Bible training institutions are not to be trusted? No way! Some are certainly better than others, but like everything in life, you'd better know enough of your Bible to separate the wheat from the chaff.

You'll never notice much holiness happening without an ample anointing of the Ruach Ha Kodesh.[8] He's the Teacher of teachers as long as you don't stop too short, hung up on one or two of the novelties of a big name instead of the hard service bit.

Nevertheless, in all depth of seriousness, from my own Third World, BBII[9] observations and doing justice to the paramount point of these pages, Gentile anti-Semitism surfaces well into the Western system of education—and not the least, in the theological tenets of Bible training.

So far we have looked at St. Augustine, St. Thomas Aquinas, Luther and Calvin—all under the heavy influence of Aristotle and the Hellenistic Masters. These four names and their origins will not always be apparent but the undercurrents of what they have represented will be there.

Their direct degradations of the Chosen Seed may not still be emphasized, but the undercurrents will be there.

It will not always be from the texts they taught, but with the mentality of a humanistic, indulgent, and self-seeking West—Anti-Semitism and a watered down deity will be there.

But the greatest quantum shift of all in these subtle alterations falls in the direction of full blown anti-Semitism. The most devastating, without question, is Replacement Theology, which comes without a truly biblical grasp of the Hebrew Scriptures. It is arrogance that the Jews "used to be" the pretty "chosen posies" but now the church has seized the moment and usurped the supposed high office of a "chosen clique." The Messiah has now been supplanted by the Gentiles actually "owning" the Messiah and by upstaging those rebellious Jews. Talk about body snatching!

It's not that the Jews have always gotten it right, but the Hebrew Scriptures are replete that the Almighty has His own personal plans to bring the body back on track at His ultimate point of ingathering. We'll return to that later.

More Shortcuts to the Kingdom

However, a close corollary to Replacement Theology is the more subtle pre-tribulation Rapture theory. You can prove the phenomenon with a clever choice of "proof texts" but not if you include *all* verses related to the matter! It is a classic collision of reality with Scripture. The church supposedly will do an ingenious Enoch-type "blaze of glory" departure while the Jews get left behind once again with one more Nazi-style déjà vu. For shame! The Hebrew prophets in my Bible do not project that upon the God-fearing, Messiah-awaiting Jew, and neither does yours.

I was taught about this fabricated fire escape for the end of days as a teenager and actually naively believed it until when in my thirties I translated the book of Revelation into the Waola language of PNG and found it all to be an anti-Semitic trap. It's not in the Good Book! Jew and Gentile are both here for the long haul—hopefully not too long anymore—each in our respective distances to the goal posts.

Challengingly, in the last few weeks of this writing with the gruesome massacres of Christians in the Middle East, anti-Semitism has become Judeo-Christian anti-Semitism, but the good news is, like Job, as our testing progresses and as the temperatures in the furnace of affliction shift: *"He knows the way that I take; when he has tested me, I will come forth as gold."*[10]

I was awakened to much more of this across five decades in a Hellenist-free Third World, absent of those hidden humanistic mental blocks that had long marginalized and undermined truth and virtue in the West.

There are numerous church-dividing theological tenets for which Scripture is largely silent, such as hard-line after-death assumptions, Replacement Theology, Pre-tribulation Rapture, Dispensationalism, and all categories of theological classifications that may have a cause for consideration but hardly a license for pouring theological presumption into concrete or chiselling it into stone.

Moses puts it well in Deuteronomy 29:29:

"The secret things belong to the LORD our God, but the things revealed belong to us and to our children forever, that we may follow all the words of this law."

Hellenism modifies it menacingly: "The secret things belong to humanistic thinkers" but by the time eager theologians get done with that one, we've forgotten what we're supposed to do in the rest of the verse!

The old maxim is that idleness is the devil's workshop. If there's a crack in the program, old Snake-Eyes will fill it. Unfortunately as with Hellenism, if there are a few spaces in the text, humanism will be there to direct the traffic!

Obviously—or it ought to be obvious—all of these untouchable "tenets of truth" can be presumptuously proven "without doubt," yet really at best, convincing only half of the crowd. And even that is only with a clever choice of text to the exclusion of not a few other Scriptures. Moreover, the starkest moment of truth of all, is that most of these clever divisive doctrinal deductions have a clandestine backdoor to anti-Jewish, anti-Semitic bigotry. It is there! And sadly it comes from so-called Christians.

Before we go on, there's one more verse we have to consider:

"...*as it is written: 'What no eye has seen, what no ear has heard, and what no human mind has conceived'—the things God has prepared for those who love him.*"[11]

Unfortunately, some of the big producers from Reformation Resources already have their flyers prepared for all the goodies Glory might give. No need to wait. With a tad of throwback to Athens, Western theology can also come up with whatever you want! Name it and claim it!

The bottom line: It is a Greek thing to worship a theology while it is a Hebraic thing to enter into a relationship with your Creator! Or even for others: It is Greek mentality to worship traditions of Truth; it is a Hebraic thing to live it.

The naive may never notice, but everyone else from the Jew to the anti-Semites themselves can either sense or use the subtlety of this bigoted bias. And it ambles from Athens to Rome and from Rome to the Reformation. It is hardly the sole reason for Jew-bashing, but it certainly sharpens Goliath's spear.

Chapter 8

Idolatry's Link to Anti-Semitism

Just to follow the flow, we began our long search for answers with ancient struggles in four dysfunctional families of the earliest of biblical records. The four scenarios included one murder, two more would be homicides and two additional conflicts that resulted into two now millennium-old diametrically opposed ideologies, including wars unending that just don't seem to disappear.[1]

Now at the first, this might appear to be a bit bizarre because should all four case-studies of family in-fighting seem to indict everyone across the same clan—this more or less might justify a bad name for any and all stereotypes—if that's what they actually were. But it should hardly generate hatred across nations.

Moreover those first four dysfunctional families melded into a people in particular that were anything but a crop of down-and-outers but rather champion winners, giant killers, geniuses, professionals, Nobel Prize laureates, and survivors across centuries.

Meanwhile their sometime contemporaries, the Hittites, the Hivites, the Jebusites, the Canaanites, the Ninevites, the Amorites, the Midianites, and a long roster of reigns of other renegades now are gone forever. And their silence in absentia is deafening.

This certainly should tell us something. On the one hand, it might be merely medieval happenings of history, but on the other, certainly not a source of anti-Semitism! Really?

True, in addition to their Daniels and their Davids, Elijahs, Elishas, and more currently their Einsteins, the Jews may have had their own bad boy or two, like an Ahab or Absalom. But why are all of them so hated and feted as the world's oldest scapegoat as well!

And all the while, anti-Semitism seeps on. Hatred breeds on, and evil is alive and festering! So what about any connection of all of this with idolatry? That's alive and well too, but not too many seem to notice it these days.

Let's have a look. Idolatry was another pesky problem that Israel had to grapple with back in the Good Old Days—or we should say the bad old bygones? The Almighty told His people through the prophets from Isaiah and Jeremiah (especially), through Ezekiel, Amos, and all the rest down through Malachi, that if they behaved themselves, they would remain in their God-deeded domain forever. But if things went derelict in the direction of apostasy and worship of the Canaanite Baal's and other godless glitter, out they'd go.

In short that dispersion has happened three times, once in a partial rout of ten of Israel's twelve tribes by the Ninevites in 722 BCE. It happened again in the expulsion of the remaining two tribes—Judah and Benjamin—by the Babylonians in 586 BCE. And then a third time, after a great number of repentant refugees had returned home to Jerusalem in subsequent eras, once again the less than Jew-loving Romans—aka pagan Rome—drove them out of Jerusalem in 70 AD all the way through to 132 AD.

Then what? And what might that have to do with the coming-of-age practice of political correctness in 2015 anyway?

And what's idolatry? Isn't that just an ancient Jewish brand of backsliding from their better behavior by copying other pagans who did religious rituals like child sacrifice, made offerings to their demonic gods, and followed retarded rituals?

As simple as we can make it, idolatry is anti-God—just like

anti-Semitism is anti-Jewish. Nevertheless, this of course may suggest that anti-Semitism is anti-God as well. For sure it is! Everything we've considered so far points to the fact that both are out of the same cookie cutter.

Here's how it works: After listing in Leviticus 18 an ample sample of perversions practiced by the Canaanites, God tells the Israelites on their way out of Egypt what they will need to know about idolatry on their return to their Land of Promise. And He lists the cause and effect upon the very real estate He Himself had created in the process.

To paraphrase His clues: "Israel, If you understand the cause and effect of Creation within the nations I've created, you'll be okay for a long while; but if you don't, out you'll go just like the Canaanites before you." And then His word "vomit" makes the point!

Here's the exact text for testing Israel's tenure from Leviticus 18:24-28:

> "Do not defile yourselves in any of these ways, because this is how the nations that I am going to drive out before you became defiled. Even the land was defiled; so I punished it for its sin, and the land vomited out its inhabitants. But you must keep my decrees and my laws. The native-born and the foreigners residing among you must not do any of these detestable things, for all these things were done by the people who lived in the land before you, and the land became defiled. And if you defile the land, it will vomit you out as it vomited out the nations that were before you."

A couple of observations, however: This is hardly just for Hebrews! It's a life principle to which the 21st century politically correct crowd has not yet awakened. I suggest you follow it up carefully in my earlier cited book in Chapter 5: *Nineveh, a Parody of the Present: Biblical Clues to the Rise and Fall of America*.[2] Across biblical history, how long do you think these various nations lasted? This is more of the same principle, along with the same warnings! The book's insight covers five ancient biblical kingdoms that had run the gauntlet—plus survival prospects on today's Europe, and of course the fast fading days of the USA. We look at how long their political tenure lasted,[3] and what they did before the Almighty finally blew the whistle.

Where Did Palestinians Come from and What Do They Worship?

But in the Middle East, there is one more most interesting twist: Some of the rag-tag remnants of those Arabs who had wandered in from various pan-Arab nations began to settle in what Roman Emperor Hadrian had renamed Falastina[4]—aka Palestine—in 132 AD.

Those who lived in what the world had dubbed Palestine had no nationality of their own and had simply been known as Arabs from across the Middle East. Militarily they were also known as *fedayeen* that are labelled on line as "Arab guerrillas operating especially in Israel and Palestine against the Israeli government; and in Iraq against the coalition forces during and after the Second Gulf War."

Before their statehood in 1948, the Jews who in the mid-1800s had begun returning to their ancient homeland following Rome's 132 AD rout of Israel aka Judea, Samaria, the Aravah and Galilee. These returning Jews were ironically the ones the nations began to call the Palestinians.

When the Jews had been recognized by the UN as a nation in their own right in 1948, they no longer needed that concocted Roman ridicule. They were Israelis! Thus, when Egyptian[5] Yasser Arafat showed up in the mid-1960s, he picked up that tattered *Palestinian* label, dusted it off, and started organizing those vagabond Arabs as *Palestinians*. Before long, their adventurous imaginations concluded that their ancestors must have actually been living there for some 5000 years, with their most ambitious claim to fame of all—that they were really the offspring of those long extinct ancient Canaanites!

Whoa, that must have been before the nomads knew there was such a thing as encyclopaedias! Better yet, they could have begun to check up in the Holy Writ had they had a copy!

The Good Book says by Creation's law of cause and effect that the Almighty ran the Canaanites off the planet—vomited them out if you recall—because of gross sexual perversion and immorality. The above paragraphs are perfect examples of the Ancient of Day's purposes of planting a garden of virtue and sanity in the midst of a mire of medieval manners and mentality.

Are the Palestinian Arabs sure they still want to be identified with those Canaanites?

Gaza Joins the Hate Chorus

As we first touched on the some 3000 rocket, terrorist barrage into Israel by Hamas aka the Palestinians back in Chapter 5—Gaza was in the throes of the 2014 war detailed earlier. It was actually a propaganda war in a matrix of Palestinian sham and political legos. Indeed, segments of truth, deception, and facts were assembled and reassembled like kindergarten construction toys to shape a pretext and fabricate a fraud to con the globe, using expendable lives—women and children—to win a media war no matter how much blood is shed.

What on earth did that Egyptian-born Arafat have to do with land-gouging credibility claiming *Palestinians* other than his leading a pan-Islamic crusade to drive the Jews into the sea? In his prime back in the 1970s, he boasted he would raise up a million martyrs—suicide terrorists—to overthrow Israel.

Children born in those days—after 10 or 12 years of watching

Palestinian children's Sesame Street-type kid's TV that taught—not fun and games—but spilling of blood and guts in hatred of the Jew. The Jew is programmed first and foremost as the thief of "Palestinian" lands, the offspring of apes and pigs, and the ultimate goal for any upstanding young Palestinian to destroy. Kill a Jew and you have your only sure guarantee of Paradise. Lovely stuff for the youngsters!

Streets, sporting, and community events are all named after suicide bombers ranked on the number of Jews they have destroyed. I kid you not! This is all taped and translated into English by key services like MEMRI,[6] CAMERA,[7] along with Palestinian Media Watch. As noted above, my files contain about 500 entries by Palestinian Media Watch, mostly from television recordings.

Perhaps you didn't know that "Jesus was a Palestinian who was murdered by the Jews because he was trying to stop them from stealing Palestinian land"! You probably wouldn't have heard that if you don't speak Arabic and don't watch kids' PA television.

The fact is quite chilling that Arafat first launched his "million martyr" boast in the 1970s and now those first such programmed kids are now in their 40s. Gaza rocket war? Tunnels? Terrorists? Go figure!

Has anyone in the UN or the European Union or the White House for that matter, ever read the Hamas Charter and/or the Palestinian Authority Charter translated from Arabic? Both identically state that the Jew in the Middle East must be totally destroyed!

Saving face is everything for Hamas; human shields are cheap, and propaganda becomes the strategic truth. We did say "media war," but the core goal is to destroy the wretched Jew forever which is nothing new from Amalek to Adolph, so obviously, it hasn't happened yet. The Prophet Jeremiah—along with all the other prophets—say it will never happen.[8] But it's a nasty irritation, and like that curse of Amalek, it won't go away.

The social media was flooded with a tsunami of sham and half-truths in the 50 days of this latest war of rockets and misrepresentations, including intensive censorship and monitoring of all international media reporting of what was actually happening to create an immense loss of life from intentionally positioning human shields in harm's way. And that was forcing many at Hamas gunpoint including all photography of political manipulations!

This was reminiscent of sorts to Joseph Stalin's former tactics with what he termed "useful idiots," but with far more senseless bloodletting by Hamas this time around.

The Hamas tactic, of course, was to effectively control all global TV propaganda, quite "sanitizing" the reports of any and all war crimes that Hamas was committing. The UN agencies and International Media, not surprisingly, had little difficulty in failing to see those breaches in accuracy, since honesty when it comes to demonizing Israel never has been a high card across most of the international community.

Remember my wife and I were here all the while!

As noted above, if the UN, the EU, and the flood of Big Media has never noticed—or cared—that the Hamas and the Palestinian Authority Charters—including the pseudo "moderates"—all call for the complete annihilation of the Jews, why should they even blink at the perverted, artificial, sleight of hand media reporting of the Gaza conflict? Moreover, all the while Islamist positioning across the Western world instigated marches and riots that were total misrepresentations of reality but completed the global display of cursing Israel once more.

Saving face, Hamas won a media battle, but on the side of reality, Israel had capped the rocket barrage for the time being. Meanwhile Hamas buried over 2100 of their forced but expendable human shields, while it will yet take a decade to rebuild and restore the collateral damage.

The jaundiced media lobbed all the carnage off onto Israel, as terrorist coffers from the Middle East will pick up the tab for much of it. Unfortunately, much will also come from Western taxpayer dollars for "Palestinian Aid." The truly needy Palestinians had little if anything to do with the travesty, while their "Aid Package" will never be touched by those actually needing it. The funds would go straight back into planning for the next round of rockets. Sorry to say, Hamas is still hatred's hideout, while the world yet again condemns Israel for the entire mayhem.

It is a curiosity that the bloodletting once again broke loose in the midst of this probe into anti-Semitism, but it is obvious to me that the Almighty had it on His agenda. Such is Israel's neighborhood, but as we search the Scriptures we find a fascinating verse in Deuteronomy 32:8:

"When the Most High gave the nations their inheritance; when he divided all mankind, he set up boundaries for the peoples according to the number of the sons of Israel."

That's an intriguing text, and if I get it right, it would suggest the Most High knew all along what He has planned for 2015 Gaza and why!

Yet before we leave their ominous neighborhood, there are a few more high hurdles for the Israeli citizens in general that we might contemplate.

First, here's one of the less scientific ones: A few years back there was a smallish strength-four earthquake in the Jordan Valley, and sure enough, the Palestinians said it was the Jews who did it! What else is new?

And then there are the historical hurdles: The Jews have had archives of recorded history across millennia, including two majestic temples and a myriad of kings and kingdoms all on pages of Holy Writ. Yet their neighbors today tweet on Twitter that the Jews only first showed their faces in the area around 1880. On top of that they say: "There is no archaeological proof whatsoever that the Jews ever had a temple in Jerusalem, nor even ever set foot in the environs prior to 1948." Unbelievable!

But There Is a Plan

God told Israel that if they stuck with Him, they'd keep their Promised Land forever—that is their Middle East heritage promised to Abraham, Isaac, and Jacob, and their offspring—otherwise out you go!

More from Leviticus 20:22:

> *"Keep all my decrees and laws and follow them, so that the land where I am bringing you to live may not vomit you out."*

And that, as we have seen, is exactly what happened!

But the Good News for any and all victims of anti-Semitism— and in particular the offspring of those one-time idolaters from the Seed of Abraham—who had lost the lease on their real estate under Creation's divine law of cause and effect. There are multiple promises in the Good Book[9] for their return, but Jeremiah says it best:

> *"I will bring Judah and Israel back from captivity, and will re- build them as they were before. I will cleanse them from all the sin they have committed against me and will forgive all their sins of rebellion against me. Then this city* [Jerusalem] *will bring me renown, joy, praise and honor before all nations on earth that hear of all the good things I do for it; and they will be in awe and will tremble at the abundant prosperity and peace I provide for it"* (Jeremiah 33:7-9).

And one more of the numerous mentions of the above regath- ering of the Jews and their return home to Israel is also worthy of mention in Isaiah 14:1-2.[10]

"But the LORD will have mercy on the descendants of Jacob. He will choose Israel as his special people once again. He will bring them back to settle once again in their own land. And people from many different nations will come and join them there and unite with the people of Israel. The nations of the world will help the people of Israel to return, and those who come to live in the Lord's land will serve them."

Sounds like even with all the poor press and nasty names in the interim, it might be worth waiting for!

Anti-Semitism and Anti-God

In reflection, have you read the 119th Psalm lately? Have you ever read it? It's an epic—all 176 verses!

In particular, it presents a unique effect. It is divided into 22 subdivisions of 8 verses per cut. But there's something distinctive about its para-message.[11] There are at least five alternating words of yearning for an invitation of bonding together with the Most High that is repeated over and over and over again. "Precepts" are used 19 times, "decrees" 19 times, "statutes" 17, "commands" 20 and "righteous laws" 8 or more.

Here's a sample of one of the 22 subdivisions:

"Your word, Lord, is eternal; it stands firm in the heavens. Your faithfulness continues through all generations; you established the earth...Your laws endure to this day, for all things serve you. If your law had not been my delight, I would have perished in my affliction. I will never forget your precepts, for by them you have preserved my life. Save me, for I am yours; I have sought out your precepts. The wicked are waiting to destroy me, but I will ponder your statutes. To all perfection I see a limit, but your commands are boundless" (Psalm 119:89-96).

Is this just a bit of legalism for a regimented routine? Hardly! Are these like dietary laws? I doubt that. Personal purity? I don't think so. Abusive speech? Not at all. Certainly any of these issues may have positive or negative values but the Psalmist uses these five-plus separate terms to affect the same unitary plea. It's simply a heart cry from five directions of the Psalmist's soul that "I crave your intimacy, Abba."

A wider grasp of his feeling is to look across those immortal Ten Commandments. The first four involve our relationship with the Most High. The last six bridge our bond with one other. Certainly they are all important, but I observe they are ranked in importance, and the very first one of all is the Head of all the rest—*"No other gods beside me!"* And it is the flouting of this first one that I am sure is cut and dried idolatry no matter what layer of hedonism those other tin gods aka idols may happen to be—for the Jew first and for all the rest of us.

So before you curse the Creator, in one of His earliest decisions of divine selection, He mused: "First off, I'll need a chosen family of foot soldiers for my human errands!" And these happened to be Hebrews, later to be known as the Jews.

So what if you're not comfortable with this? This is simply a pilot project for the entirety of all humanity. With all of Creation's clay, suppose that had He labelled the chosen few as French, we all know that the results would have been no different!

Be forewarned. You're part of the trial run! We all are. You may or may not be one of the foot soldiers. But you *are on* the service roster—and being monitored at that!

Anti-Semitism is but a Siamese twin to anti-God. Remember the first four fractured families? "Why did you create me into this 2nd class status?" Anti-God and more! And anti-God even drags a bit of anti-Semitism along with it.

From those former families, we went through to a window into personal complaining—"This manna ain't bread, where's the meat?"

"Moses, you're a dictator in this whole thing"; or to the Prophet Samuel: "We need a king!" And then on to Constantine and on to those Western Wonder Wizards from the Athens Academy. And finally in the course of time, "Hey, everybody knows it is the Jews who are responsible for this whole mess!"

Remember back at the end of Chapter One regarding those five one-word questions in quest of wisdom: Who? How? Where? When? and Why? I suggest the most purposeful probe of all must be Why? Why is there such hatred against the Jew? Why is the Jew blamed for everything from earthquakes to trying to survive terrorists? Is the Jew always the culprit? Or is it really the One who created him for a test run—running errands?—an envoy for the King? A channel to the Messiah!

Idolatry—anti-God—seemed to have been the biggest snare across the ancient ages for even the foot soldier team. It was precisely identified as following the Canaanite gods. But the Canaanites are no more, are they?

Do you suppose that any Chosen Servant—Jew or Gentile—could be seen as a symbolic parallel today when getting off of life's starting blocks on the wrong foot? I reckon it may have possibilities. We'll check it out in the next chapter.

Anti-Semitism is but a Siamese twin to anti-God.

Chapter 9

Idols in the Closet—Idols on Display

So far we've scanned the global stage to survey the world's oldest hatred—detesting the despicable Jew! The disease of verbal degradation of anything Jewish is now pandemic: "The Jews have gobbled down everything, and they goofed up everything else! They have all the money, they master the media, and they cause all the wars. Everything is their fault!"

How blind, biased, and bigoted can the human species get!

But then we pulled the curtain back just enough to peek backstage and discover that anti-Semitism had also been the juvenile delinquent playmate of anti-God. Together they grew up into God hatred. Moreover, there's not much love lost anywhere—villainy is villainy and venom is venom.

In fact that's the exact essence of Darren Aronofsky's recent *Noah* film about the Great Flood. He shows how the "cruel Creator" is behind this gargantuan genocide of a global Flood, and nebulous Noah plays His henchmen. Hope you didn't waste your time, money, and decency in seeing it. It was the mirror image of morality—biblical characters but where left becomes right and right becomes left.

Aronofsky—being raised in a conservative Jewish background—it's not hard to connect the dots to sense a rejection of one's real roots to be able to cast the Creator as a genocidal culprit against humanity. Sadly, there are such things as self-hating Jews. Consequently, with a blockbuster like that aimed to mesmerize a godless humanity, who needs a chapter on idolatry? Nevertheless, we'll try.

One thing I have discovered in my lengthening lifetime is that the closer that a usurper may get to a pretense of the *real* truth—the farther he actually veers from his coveted kudos. It's like some preachers and their parishes, denominations and their dogma, or theologians and their theories, for instance, who make a goal of goodness and sadly end up just the opposite. Some would presume to have found a panacea for everything from musical member-ship—aka musical chairs—to crusty cults, plus their guarantee to offer you heaven done up with a pretty pink bow. Watch it! Usually such claims can slip a cog in the search engine, and the sought-after side effect of sanctity gets totally crashed into cyberspace.

Playing God

One of the major temptations in this regard is a church leader, maybe it's alternately even a rabbi, and for sure, a few of those big names in TV evangelism who have succumbed to "playing God." Unfortunately it happens all too often. You can't get into idolatry any faster or deeper than with a spiritual superiority syndrome!

Our athletic coach in high school had a little notice on our dressing room bulletin board: "The bigger a man's head gets, the easier it is to fill his shoes."

Unhappily, once some of the fellows—or ladies perhaps—get entrenched into the system, you can't get them out! They're glued into their position, but you're the one that gets stuck! And you don't even have to be a pseudo-Christian to play the game. I men-tioned rabbis above, but the phenomenon could creep into any level of civil leadership. So that's really going down—hardly up—the Totem Pole.

As I recall, checking out those totem poles should also remind us a bit of the graven image Commandments of biblical insights, so that also could well be a major point of the metaphor! This I'm-like-God-game[1] could infect the CEO of any system. CEOs may be a bit lower in the "holiness" rank than the theological hierarchy but no less vulnerable. Look, some of the corporate climbers may not even know what the Good Book says about humility. Even parents—Mom and Dad or maybe Mom or Dad—can act the role—but never grandparents as I remember!

Of course, parents are God-appointed guardians of our children but in today's godless generation, it's very easy to miss a beat in the tempo of the times and try to duplicate the Deity instead of getting our hands a bit worn and wrinkled from the wet clay on that potter's wheel. That is, we should be molding pliable clay instead of driving a stage coach!

Collective Sanctified Idolatry

But there is even more idolatry in life than individual religious titans trying to upstage the Almighty with their personal authority. Another affront involving the Holy Writ is a collective or communal effort that we have also observed over the years. That is, the Pharisees who are far more spiritual—or possibly theologically in tune—than the Sadducees.

Now that hardly refers to those original competitors from the synagogues of yesteryear, but there are those sanctified species of our day who have morphed into Christianity and who major in upstaging. With them I think we're still viewing actors on a symbolic stage. Then there's all the other shams who claim that it is their taste buds alone that follow the true faith.

That's not to say there are no other frauds—they are legion—but it is to say that there are far more idolaters when it comes to flaunting one's pedigree in parish principles. So pride and performance is a major pitfall to pastor, priest, and parishioner alike, and the larger the community, the stickier it can get. Please be assured I am hardly addressing the multitudes of bona fide religious affiliates; however, spiritual pride is perhaps the slipperiest slope of all for self-generated idolatry.

Moses and the Rock Stars

Dropping down a rung from those more spiritual Titans, we have the obvious host of performing champions of Entertainers 2014-2015 which includes Rock Idols. Yet these are never to be confused with the Rock miracles of Moses and the ancients. Of a certainty, some Rocks do have higher ratings than others. And for sure Moses rocked to the beat of a quite different Drummer! So here's the real bedrock of Moses in Exodus 17:3, 5-7:

> *"But the people were thirsty for water there, and they grumbled against Moses. They said, 'Why did you bring us up out of Egypt to make us and our children and livestock die of thirst?' The Lord answered Moses, 'Go out in front of the people. Take with you some of the elders of Israel and take in your hand the staff with which you struck the Nile, and go. I will stand there before you by the rock at Horeb. Strike the rock, and water will come out of it for the people to drink.' So Moses did this in the sight of the elders of Israel. And he called the place Massah and Meribah because the Israelites quarrelled and because they tested the Lord saying: 'Is the Lord among us or not?'"*

As noted near the beginning of Chapter 6, this miracle of striking the Rock in the Wilderness was cited some sixteen times between Exodus and Deuteronomy. The name Rock was frequently being capitalized by the translators as well as also being symbolically referred to as the Angel of the Lord who at times went ahead of this massive people-movement, and at other times moving behind as their rear guard.

Or there was even Peter's star Rock declaration in Caesarea Philippi[2] for that matter.

But those down-to-earth Rock stars have far more competition these days, and worshipping them is front page priority with unabashed recognition of their status on the success ladder. There are Rock idols on TV, YouTube Idols, and Tinsel town Idols, also Footie[3] Idols and NBA Idols plus millions more. There is no end to the celebrities who are worshipped across the Western World, and this is hardly a condemnation if someone has been an achiever and he or she is highly respected and well liked. That's quite another category to be measured on its own.

Look, I'm not a nerd. I'm a lover of sports from way back. I like Australian Rugby and most other sports; You Tube has a lot to contribute. Except for *Fiddler on the Roof,* I can do without most of Hollywood. But none of that should hold top spot or even near.

Worship is worship is worship, and there is Someone we all know from Outer Space who is very sensitive about who and what we worship. Humankind can do a lot of things wrong from Hedonism and perverted sex to dancing with the devil, but worship is a red line of priority never to be crossed. Obviously it may be far, far too late in the day to declare this in the Western World, but facts are facts, worship is worship and idolatry is idolatry.

Idolatry is when you or I give anything priority over our relationship with our Creator. That's very simple, but may be a bit difficult in these days of humanism that presents a massive competition with the Most High. And if He's not the Most High, that means your bar is set too low.

Moreover, you and I are not here to be entertained. I'm here on assignment and I'd suppose truth-be-told, we all should be. Indeed, the world we now live in has long lost the plot.

Martyr Jim Elliot, massacred by the Auca Indians of Ecuador in 1956, left behind the memorable and treasured motto: "He is no fool who gives what he cannot keep for that which he cannot lose."

I'd say that's pretty much the inverse of idolatry. And all of the above chapter from pride and power to the pit is no more or no less than anti-God.

Anti-God is a corollary of anti-Semitism, and the above is not a nit-picking judgment of a globe gone crazy with gimmickry, glitter, and gluttony but a world that has lost its way in a forest of fantasy, fiction, and failure. It's idolatry pure and simple. Yet it's even more than wasted time on fun and games.

Even a longing lure for retirement has a lingering lust for luxury at last. I knew a dear soul of days gone by that defined retirement as getting new tires and roaring back on the road. And if I get all four flats, it's time to get back to Abba and ask Him where He wants me to *walk* next!

Worshipping BAAL Today

You thought that Baal was a Canaanite god, didn't you? Well, it used to be, but it's my new acronym for today's measurement for mastery of success. Not everyone is frittering their time away, reaching for a stardom that may never pay them in cash.

How about modern BAAL worship standing for Banking, Accrued Assets, and Liquidity? We're now switching to one other major idol worshipped globally, which is that battle for the big bucks. Of course, one has to realize that any takings will have to be cast into concrete before the predicted soon coming crash, and even then, worship of worldly wealth has its limitations. I understand that all the goodies that were tucked into the sarcophagi[4] of those ancient king-types entombed in the Pyramids of Egypt were barely used when they dug into them. That seems like a bit of a waste!

Did you ever wonder why Egypt had so many garage sales—just kidding, of course—but I'm not less than serious when I say you can't take it with you! Actually this is not merely my retarded responses. Someone much wiser in investments than I am, long ago

95

suggested a more superior value system than what is presently politically popular. He's recorded in Luke 12:15:

> *"Then he said to them, 'Watch out! Be on your guard against all kinds of greed; life does not consist in an abundance of possessions.'"*

And there is one more meditation on the matter in Matthew 24:37-39:

> *"As it was in the days of Noah, so it will be at the coming of the Son of Man. For in the days before the flood, people were eating and drinking, marrying and giving in marriage up to the day Noah entered the ark; and they knew nothing about what would happen until the flood came and took them all away. That is how it will be at the coming of the Son of Man."*

That was a bit of the Bible it seems Noah's film director, Aronofsky, might have overlooked.

One other thing that some of us also might have missed about the most secure investment on the planet—there's a lot of hungry people out there that are desperate for food. You'll never lose investing in that one!

I am hearing from more and more people that are mutually aware that we are living in unprecedented days—unprecedented for us at least—and that it's long past time to search for more stable underpinnings than in the past! So much for the Golden Calf [5] revisited.

The Lone Ranger of the Wild West

Then there's the idolatry of "my preference"— what I want. It's another idolatry of selfish egoism, much of a no-brainer! And it's rife, not across the old western cowboys and Indians frontier, but it's endemic today across an individualist Western way of life. Don't forget where humanism came from, and whose culture it was that brought us that Hellenist value system! We might go to a university and far beyond to learn what others have discovered the hard way. These days the self-styled individualist can appease his abysmal appetite for an alternative to sanity with most any abomination he or she chooses. That picks up on slogging the hard way alright—but alas, without adding any smarts to the suckers who fall for the system. Willful, wild, and woefully wrong are they, but none the wiser!

Was worshipping idols ever any more intelligent than pretending to prosper from independent preferences? It doesn't pay— and it certainly has a short shelf life!

We have a bit of biblical wisdom on this one as well from Paul the Apostle in 1 Cor 6:12-13:

"'I have the right to do anything,' you say—but not everything is beneficial. 'I have the right to do anything'—but I will not be mastered by anything. You say, 'Food for the stomach and the stomach for food, and God will destroy them both.' The body, however, is not meant for sexual immorality but for the Lord, and the Lord for the body."

The success-sponsor that penned this bit of insight also shared with us a little of his own off-shore Graduate Studies that put him on the trip of a lifetime for anyone eager for over-the-moon experiences, No druggie could keep up with his brand of ecstasy! And he even ended up with the honor of being executed by Rome's top troops. Here's a bit of his bio:

"Are they Hebrews? So am I. Are they Israelites? So am I. Are they Abraham's descendants? So am I...I have been in prison more frequently...flogged more severely ...exposed to death again and again. Five times I received from the (authorities) forty lashes minus one. Three times I was beaten with rods, once

*I was pelted with stones, three times I was shipwrecked, I spent
a night and a day in the open sea, I have been constantly on the
move. I have been in danger from rivers, in danger from ban-
dits, in danger from my fellow Jews, in danger from Gentiles;
in danger in the city, in danger in the country, in danger at sea;
and in danger from false believers. I have...toiled and have
often gone without sleep; I have known hunger and thirst and
have often gone without food; I have been cold and naked.
Besides everything else, I face daily the pressure of my concern
for all the churches.*"[6]

Talk about a genuine Lone Ranger but one with a vision for
helping others! And that even without any "Silver" as a backup![7]

There are two reasons for choosing to be different. One is a
form of self-worship by being your own private god, master, and
self-manufactured miracle, aka misfit. You do nothing the hard
way. And you gain nothing for it in return. A bed of spikes may
prove a point—a lot of points in fact! What's the real point?

The other route is a moral choice of a value system with the ultimate honor of being right. Like Paul, the hard way might even be
harder. Was he crazy? A loopy loser? No way! He was a super-
achiever on assignment from the King. Picking up on the challenge
of his people goals over a rugged road, he had not one regret for his
wild ride. He would have done it again. In retrospect, here's what
he had to sum it up:

*"I have fought a good fight, I have finished my course, I have
kept the faith."*[8]

And there are as many other idols out there as there are
demons to deify them. Doing drugs is obviously a dead end, and
hedonism—the pursuit of pleasure and sensual self-indulgence—
has its limited shot at a setting sun.

Foreign substances inhaled into the lungs, ingested into the body, or injected into the bloodstream all have the effect of temporarily heightened physical sensations but ultimately shortened longevity. Perverted sexual activity is much the same with a similar price tag of pain including AIDS that also destroys the innocent in the crossfire. Such is physical performance which includes statistics that can be Googled. For the after-death side of the coin, the stats are kept elsewhere to be reviewed later!

Idolatry is a yardstick kept over any and all of human physical behaviors as well as spiritual attitudes. And just as this is related to a rebellion against Creation and a Creator, a mindset of anti-God response is also a corollary of anti-Semitism.

Moreover, whether you've ever thought about it or not, both Jew and Gentile are guilty of exhibiting some form of anti-Semitism[9] from Cain to Constantine to Calvin and beyond. But we also have an anti-God attitude with some of the same participants from the Garden to Amalek[10] to Gaza. Perhaps we can put this all together in the next chapter and decide on who or what is responsible for runaway anti-Semitism—and maybe even the "Why."

"He is no fool who gives
what he cannot keep
for that which he cannot lose."
–Jim Elliot

Chapter 10

Where and Why the Book Began

Just over a year ago[1] I had been enrolled at Yad Vashem, the Living Holocaust Memorial in Jerusalem for those six million Jews, gassed, shot and incinerated by Adolph Hitler's genocidal minions. Much of the study program focused on anti-Semitism but dealt primarily with documented instances of bigotry and hatred toward the Jews across the board. As I recall, the reasons behind the perversion presented in the course were not given as much focus as the facts on the ground.

One of our lecturers acknowledged, "We don't have any specific date for the birthday of anti-Semitism." Instantaneously a prompt into my spirit from the Heavenlies—a whisper so familiar to many in this land of the Living Word—that said, "But you do!" It was clear, specific, and stark, and has been indelible in my consciousness to this day!

"I do?" was my spontaneous deliberation.

Memory flashed back across my recollections of the past. Indeed, I knew that basically all biblical record of humanity's responses to the Creator actually surfaced in Genesis 3.

"Now the serpent was more crafty than any of the wild animals the Lord God had made. He said to the woman, 'Did God really say, "You must not eat from any tree in the garden'?"

But the Ruach[2] added one additional whisper: "Better write that down in a book." My automated reflection to that was, *Hineni*—"Here am I, send me" which was the precise utterance in Hebrew by Isaiah in Chapter 6 of his prophetic account.[3]

I have struggled not a few times since whether I should have responded so quickly with knee-jerk reaction. But I did and here I am telling you about it!

And following through with my de-facto compliance, we have thus far looked at symbolic variations of anti-Semitism in those first four families of biblical history. Much of this was not directly anti-Semitic but actually dissatisfaction with the Father's decisions!

We saw collective complaining against the Creator in the wilderness journey and again complaints toward God-appointed leadership for His Chosen Servants. We saw Gentile jealousy because of their missing-the-cut of chosenness. And we saw, as well, the substitution of Gentile "improvements" to steer the theological ship, or even in democratically replacing heaven with humanism.

We considered the gamut of grievances against an out-of-reach God deemed a despot with a supposedly out-of-date system to run His cosmos. We saw that rebellion reigned alike in both Jew and non-Jew. But we also saw that some of the Goyim[4] outsiders were impressed enough with the Father of Creation and His decisions for human destiny that they also wanted to climb on board with the Chosen Few. And they were welcomed with a true Father's genuine compassion!

Thus we likewise had to conclude that anti-Semitism was a corollary of anti-God. Amid much of the mischief is the stark inability to kick the Creator, so the crude alternative was to cowardly crush His kids—both observant and even non-observant Jews and now even the Christian come-alongs.

Consequently, the rest of this chapter will finish off with a lot of Bible to fill all the cracks and provide a complete picture of the ongoing problem that plagues the faithful.

Facing the Facts across a Kaleidoscope of Testing

Life is a kaleidoscope that is anything but a child's amusement piece. It definitely is an object lesson to demonstrate how to expect the unexpected. It is especially apropos to anti-Semitism that can come at any time and from anyplace. It will not go away. It's up and down, and down and up. It is sin, and it is a test. It is the high-hurdles of life. We run. We train. And we strive to win.

As we have noted, those bigots who live by brainless backlash would be kicking the King of Creation were their legs that long. But they're not. So they tread upon His followers. But these rebels cannot win.

Back to the Garden of tasty fruit but also tantalizing temptations, the most significant follow-on text of fruit picking is Genesis 3:15:

> *"And I will put enmity between you and the woman, and between your offspring and hers; he will crush your head, and you will strike his heel."*

Clearly, not only was the Creator central in the aftereffects of the first testing of the trio in the Garden arena, but He set the parameters of the punishment that was ongoing. The offspring of the woman was to be forever on guard, and it was the evil inclinations of a decadent humanity that was behind it all. God allows it, and a rebellious humanity is right behind!

And this is the precise time to mention not only Jewish debasement in the firing line but persecution of portions of Christianity as well. Furthermore, the attacks were not only upon Jews, but alternately from fellow Jews as well as from pagans. Let us never forget that when the facts are all in, it is not always against the actual ethnic syndrome, but anti-God wrath emanating from the demonic brood of the serpent.

Included in the Christian victimization, in John 15:19, Yeshua told His disciples:

"If you belonged to the world, it would love you as its own. As it is, you do not belong to the world, but I have chosen you out of the world. That is why the world hates you."

Then again in his intercessory prayer of John 17, Yeshua prays to the one and only Father, for the disciples and all Christians who would follow, to be rescued from the serpent's world system. John 17:14-21:

"I have given them your word and the world has hated them, for they are not of the world any more than I am of the world. My prayer is not that you take them out of the world but that you protect them from the evil one. They are not of the world, even as I am not of it. Sanctify them by the truth; your word is truth. As you sent me into the world, I have sent them into the world....My prayer is not for them alone. I pray also for those who will believe in me through their message, that all of them may be one, Father, just as you are in me and I am in you. May they also be in us so that the world may believe that you have sent me."

With all respect to my Jewish brethren who have a major problem with any actual relationship between Yeshua and the Father, be it understood that those who did follow Yeshua in believing in the one and only one Father God as Creator of the Universe, were under no less threat from the serpent as was their fellow Jew.

Unfortunately, too many Christians, but certainly not all, do snuggle within the serpent's coils against the hated Jew. Nevertheless, sorry to say there are also not a few self-hating Jews—particularly in these days of political posturing—who likewise curl up within the slippery coils of the serpent striking at any presumed Creator.

Denying any Divinity exists including His promises to the patriarchs, the chosenness of a servant community, and a biblical blueprint across eternity, those self-hating magnates of materialism delight in defying their own calling. They will support and fund any and all enemies of their own people, their lands, and their heritage. Presumably this is ethnic vitriol of sorts but quite in reverse gear. The "Cains" of Creation are still alive and kicking their own brothers!

The bottom line is that *"striking the heel"* as in Genesis 3:15 above, is not strategically against humanity—Jew or Gentile—but against the Most High himself. As we have seen, anti-Semitism is basically against God.

Ironically as I write, the greatest issue in the political arena at this particular moment in time has shifted from a nuclear Iran, a militaristic Russia, or even a resurrected Caliphate to the nearly unprecedented crucifixion, decapitation, and expulsion of Middle East Christians from their homelands across millennia of Christian inhabitation.

Again there is a nebulous "why?" Why is there such an indifferent and calloused response of Western Christianity toward their butchered and banished brethren in the present fulfilment of the biblical prophecy:[5] *"...tribulation such as never was and never will be again."*

But why, why, why? It's simple!

It's the Father, not His Family, That's the Problem

As most of Christianity had never shared as much of the emotional pain suffered among their Jewish brethren, and much of Judaism never nursed the same kind of villainy cast against their genuine Christian counterparts, so it is today of Western Christians versus Eastern Christians across their own internal man-made barriers.

Recently a US Senator, Ted Cruz, was literally driven off his lecture stage in Washington, DC and blatantly booed out of town when he noted his appreciation of and respect for Israel to a group of Eastern Christians. They went ballistic! Why? Old Snake-Eyes is a con-artist when it comes to rupturing relationships!

The Western world may care not one whit for their so-called Christian counterparts in the Middle East because the East's understanding is totally tainted by Islamic deception and fundamentalist propaganda used against both the Jew and the Middle East Christian—at alternate times and strategically swapped settings to be sure!

Unfortunately this political slander serves to cut the Eastern Church off from an identity with the same Father God in whom both East and West supposedly believe.

Thus, to the West, the East is not real Christianity; these people are different, and so who cares? Not surprisingly, the response is no different from East to West!

To the bigot, ethnicity is handy and useful in coordinating and propagating hatred.[6] Therefore, it is the core of the contempt driven by anti-Semitism. Actually it is the bigot's pride, greed, jealousy, selfishness, and supposed superiority that is central to his bad behavior.

These principles arouse a universal demonic contempt against an ordered, sovereign, and disciplined King of the Universe who is out of range of the fury of the serpent, while the King's faithful foot soldiers—Jew or adopted Gentile—are not.

And even Senator Cruz gets spit upon and taunted all the way back to Texas!

All who may represent the offspring of the seed of the woman[7]—though they may have not generally recognized themselves as such—are under a sovereign testing to monitor what they are made of, and for what purpose? We need some more Bible right now.

Testing One, Two, Three

The Almighty's testing of His Chosen Servants—foot soldiers—is a groundswell across the Hebrew Scriptures. Abraham was tested with the offering of Isaac.[8] In the Torah there are several references to testing in the Wilderness, including reviews in the Ketuvim[9] such as in Psalm 66:10: *"For you, God, tested us; you refined us like silver."*

And another in Proverbs 27:21: *"The crucible for silver and the furnace for gold, but people are tested by their praise."*

Finally into the Prophets, Isaiah continued to address refinement of the faithful in Isaiah 48:10: *"See, I have refined you, though not as silver; I have tested you in the furnace of affliction."*

The most familiar I should think is the classic in Job 23:10. *"But he knows the way that I take; when he has tested me, I will come forth as gold."*

Though in a much shorter period of testing than those observant Hebrews across the ancients—the New Testament faithful to the Father are addressed in James 1:2-5:

> *"Consider it pure joy, my brothers and sisters, whenever you face trials of many kinds, because you know that the testing of your faith produces perseverance. Let perseverance finish its work so that you may be mature and complete, not lacking anything. If any of you lacks wisdom, you should ask God, who gives generously to all without finding fault, and it will be given to you."*

We need to keep in mind, of course, that those addressed were certainly not Goyim but out and out Jews whose creed had never shifted from the Shema of Deuteronomy 6:4-8:

> *"Hear, O Israel: The Lord our God, the Lord is one. Love the Lord your God with all your heart and with all your soul and with all your strength. These commandments that I give you*

today are to be on your hearts. Impress them on your children. Talk about them when you sit at home and when you walk along the road, when you lie down and when you get up. Tie them as symbols on your hands and bind them on your foreheads. Write them on the doorframes of your houses and on your gates."

Moreover, the Apostle Peter in both of his letters directed to his brethren in the Messianic congregations, repeatedly addresses their suffering and struggles in the face of a godless and pagan world. But again, we must emphasize that those being addressed were all Jews suffering for their own personal faith in the Almighty.

The Almighty never answers to theology... theology always must answer to God.

Chapter 11

The Show's Not Over
Till the Big Gal Sings

Little did the secular crowd of the mid 20th century that immortalized the colloquialism—"The show's not over till the Big Gal sings"[1]—realize its perpetual significance, but with all due honor to our good friends, who carry an extra kilo or two, who cares? The idiom really carries an eternal warning to the would-be wise, against blind and overzealous confidence. It's both outside the box and inside the center of that Hebraic circle spiralling upward.

The Agenda Mentality

Yeshua said a few times that *"He who endures to the end shall be saved."*[2]

Also: *"In the world you shall have tribulation but I have overcome the world."*[3]

Apostle John quoted him again in Revelation to the church of Ephesus: *"Remember the height from which you have fallen—repent!"*[4] He spoke again to the church of Philadelphia: *"I will also keep you from the hour of trial that will come on the whole earth."*[5]

Yet all the while an over-casual ecclesia was euphemizing it: "If you say the right words, we've got the panacea, and you can enjoy the party!" Or "All you need is our flawless theological formula and then fill up on the fun."

While on the far side of the room, after endurance of his life-long faithfulness, Job says, *"Though he slay me, yet will I trust him."*[6]

And on the same side of that venue of verdict, Jeremiah spoke of the "usurpers" who in their arrogance have self-righteously judged the Jews without "walking the walk" in Jewish sandals:

> *"This is what the Lord says: 'As for all my wicked neighbors who seize the inheritance I gave my people Israel, I will up-root them from their lands and I will uproot the people of Judah from among them...And if they learn well the ways of my people and swear by my name, saying, 'As surely as the Lord lives'—even as they once taught my people to swear by Baal—then they will be established among my people. But if any nation does not listen, I will completely uproot and destroy it,' declares the Lord"* (Jeremiah 12:14-17).

And Yeshua also challenged both Jew and Goyim with that more than familiar: *"Judge not that you be not judged"* (Matthew 7:1-2).

Then Ezekiel also scopes out both sides of the chamber in 33:18-19:

> *"If a righteous person turns from their righteousness and does evil, they will die for it. And if a wicked person turns away from their wickedness and does what is just and right, they will live by doing so."*

And one more classic from the famous faith chapter in Hebrews 11, we find a long list of the faithful all the way from Abraham across a host of Hebrew victims, to eventually include the martyrs of verses 35-38:

"Women received back their dead, raised to life again. There were others who were tortured, refusing to be released so that they might gain an even better resurrection. Some faced jeers and flogging, and even chains and imprisonment. They were put to death by stoning; they were sawed in two;[7] they were killed by the sword. They went about in sheepskins and goatskins, destitute, persecuted and mistreated; the world was not worthy of them. They wandered in deserts and mountains, living in caves and in holes in the ground."

Thus, may I remind you that all of these were all God-fearing Jews waiting for those Gentile converts to eventually tag along as in the following two verses below:

"These were all commended for their faith, yet none of them received what had been promised, since God had planned something better for us so that only together with us would they be made perfect" (Hebrews 11:39-40).

One Redemption—Two Timetables

Unfortunately not a few Gentiles—thanks to cheerleaders like Aristotle and Hellenist chums—might be a bit surprised by the above text, but these were not quite the Gentile converts that were waiting for the Almighty to overturn the Hebraic system. These were Jews waiting for the Goyim to join those Chosen Servants—the Chosen foot soldiers that were in the eternal plan, not to just believe in—but to bring in—the promised Messiah. Consider, that those in the waiting room in Hebrews 11 were all Jews!

Thanks—but no thanks—to our friends like Augustine and Thomas Aquinas plus their follow-on's—Luther and Calvin—including a bit of their Hellenistic influence that never made it to the drycleaners! Thus, there are eye openers like the stark warning to the Goyim about the Root of the symbolic Hebraic Olive Tree of Romans 11:17-21:

"If some of the branches [Jewish] have been broken off, and you, though a wild olive shoot [Gentile], have been grafted in among the others and now share in the nourishing sap from the olive root, do not consider yourself to be superior to those other branches [Jewish]. If you do, consider this: You [Gentiles] do not support the root, but the root supports you. You will say then, 'Branches were broken off so that I could be grafted in.' Granted. But they were broken off because of unbelief, and you stand by faith. Do not be arrogant, but tremble. For if God did not spare the natural branches, he will not spare you either.

And this blends exactly hand in glove with the follow on in Romans 11:25-27:

"For I do not desire, brethren, that you should be ignorant of this mystery, lest you should be wise in your own opinion, that blindness in part has happened to Israel until the fullness of the Gentiles has come in. And so all Israel will be saved, as it is written: The Deliverer will come out of Zion, and He will turn away ungodliness from Jacob; for this is My covenant with them, when I take away their sins."

As I repeatedly note, these verses are also in your Bible as well as mine. There is one and one only atonement in place for entry into the Kingdom. Only one!

But there is more than one timetable as declared in the above text in Romans: *"blindness in part..."*; *"...until fullness of the Gentiles..."*; *"...redemption of Israel...when I take away their sins!"* How clear can you get? The God of Israel has more than one timetable on His agenda!

What say we have another witness or two for our two or three principle? The ultimate one is in Ezekiel 36:24-28:

"For I will take you out of the nations; I will gather you from all the countries and bring you back into your own land. I will

111

*sprinkle clean water on you, and you will be clean; I will
cleanse you from all your impurities and from all your idols. I
will give you a new heart and put a new spirit in you; I will
remove from you your heart of stone and give you a heart of
flesh. And I will put my Spirit in you and move you to follow
my decrees and be careful to keep my laws. Then you will live in
the land I gave your ancestors; you will be my people, and I will
be your God."*

Almost sounds like a John 3:16 conversion!

And there are at least a dozen more—parts of which we have
already quoted—that combine to say the same thing: A timetable
for the Gentiles, a timetable for the Jews! Yet all have the same one
road to atonement cum redemption.

Moreover, keep tab on the above Ezekiel 36 quotation. We'll
be referring back to it twice more before we finish the chapter.

The Goal Post Replacement Regiment

Therefore, some of the Gentiles presumed to replace the
Hebrew Scriptures with their edited Hellenist herald of hiccups. If
they read the Holy Writ at all, they did not read enough. They
blew it on two counts.

First the Jews had been chosen not as an elite entity for the
Cushy Club, but rather to take a bit of flack as faithful foot soldiers
for their King. Sorry to say, somewhere down the line being chosen
sounded so important that certain of the Goyim thought they
should have some share of the attention too!

Now that's possible and even commendable provided the
proper channels of enlistment are followed. The rear door is not
recommended, however there is a foot soldier enlistment office
right near the well-known Olive Tree Branch whose Registrar, I
understand, *neither slumbers nor sleeps.*

And the second count was that before you knew it, there were
too many chiefs lined up and not enough Indians, whereas the

Olive Tree Office had been looking more for chosen servants than trainees for Supreme Court judges!

Alternatively, I understand that enlistment is easier across the Garden at the Lemon Tree Goal Post Replacement Services. I can't say I recommend going that root, however.[8]

That may be a bit of an over-simplification, but in reality the *outsiders* from those slaves all the way back to the departure from Egypt on into New Testament times were always welcome to join the Jewish overcomers awaiting their Messiah. Sadly humanism, even up to recent times, sees the wrong side of opportunity and is all too willing to move the goal posts and take over.

Hellenistic Hangovers with Humanistic Headaches

Remember, we illustrated back in Chapter 6 that the unique articulation of the Creator and Designer of the universe has one and only one tense, NOW, and that a timeline of eternity is not from A to B in a straight line? And also remember that eternity has no beginning and no end? And that's not from anyone's rocket science handbook.

Outside of our solar system there is no designated sun, moon, or stars to set our watches, check our clocks, or adjust our calendars. What is more, the Good Book reinforces the fact that we could expect significant variations in cosmic views from those non- planet-earth locations. Things will look different, I can assure you. Beyond that, this should also help us understand what that eternal NOW is all about and a bit more insight on no beginning and no end.

"The sun will no more be your light by day, nor will the brightness of the moon shine on you, for the Lord will be your everlasting light, and your God will be your glory. Your sun will never set again, and your moon will wane no more; the Lord will be your everlasting light, and your days of sorrow will end."[9]

And Hebraically, we again repeat that we have described it, not as Greek thinking with a beginning-to-end timeline from A to B, but as an ever rising spiral into the heavenlies. May I also suggest that the atonement came not as the midpoint of a straight line, but in the indeterminate center of that ever rising spiral of redeemed humanity? Adam therefore *is*—not was—on it, and the final Jewish ingathering *is*—not will be—at Messiah's long-awaited appearance at the ingathering of Israel's exiles as detailed in the Ezekiel 36 reference above.

This is not to say that the Jew or anyone else has an alternative route into the New Jerusalem. But harking back to those two parallel previous texts—that is, Romans 11 and Ezekiel 36—along with a host of others, declare unequivocally that even though there is one and only one Redemption for humankind, there does happen to be two timetables!

And this includes at least a dozen similar references in the prophets of the ultimate ingathering of a redeemed Israel via the one and only atonement across the Hebrew Scriptures. This also could settle the muddied waters between Jew and Goyim of whether the Messiah has come yet or not. He's always been in the midst of the Creator's eternal NOW.

As we considered back in Chapter 6, in the Father's way of looking at His eternal NOW, the Messiah has been around and serving—clandestine or otherwise—since Creation! He was some 30 times biblically associated as the shielding Rock of the Exodus journey. In other contexts, the association would have been as the Angel of the Lord or, on other references in the Psalms and many of the prophets, simply as a unique Presence of God's power totalling a similar number of occurrences.

And then to many, he also posed an identity crisis with mysterious Melchizedek[10] who served bread and wine to Abraham. And he even showed up for another time or two on disputed interpretations between Jew and Gentile in the New Testament, but we

114

won't get into that one at this point in the story![11] I know—this one-tense thing may be a bit hard to get one's head around. But if some believers can see it, we all can!

Aristotle, Plato, and pals couldn't do it, so instead they had to change the times and the seasons![12] But if we're satisfied that it's something the Ancient of Days figured out, it should be okay. And as I have looked into the variations of tenses in the languages around the globe, it can and does make sense.

Look, I'm surely not saying all the Christian theologians got it wrong, but many were unfortunately influenced by Constantine cum parts of the Reformation. And there were some oversights, especially on this timeline business. By the same token, the Rabbinate from the Maccabees to modernity was anything but flawless either.

Back in Chapter 7 under the sub-heading: "Leaks in the Pipeline," we saw that under Hellenistic Greek influence on theologians Augustine and Thomas Aquinas—and consequently on into the Reformation—the potential for change from a Hebraic mindset to a Hellenistic world view was unreal. Again it has been more cultural interpretation than theological twisting, though there was also some of that as well.

The biggest hang-up is that the Hellenists have convinced the church, the pagans, and most of the rest of the party that with the last breath—that's it! It's all over! Show me where you found that in the Bible! I've searched the Holy Writ from cover to cover, and it's not there. That is a Hellenistic Greek concept!

In the Hebrew Scriptures there is a repeat concept of the departed resting with their fathers, while in the New Testament, the nearest approach is Hebrews 9:27 and *The Message* version of the Bible says it best: *"Everyone has to die once and then face the consequences."*

The atonement—aka redemption—though certainly in focus during the Christian era, was also already in place at the beginning of Creation—considering the Father's eternal NOW! Disciplinary decisions changed the land tenancy—the plan didn't.

And it was in place for unbelieving Thomas[13] when confronted in John 20:27:

> *Then he* [Yeshua] *said to Thomas, "Put your finger here; see my hands. Reach out your hand and put it into my side..."*

The doubting disciple declined doing that suggested patient check, but without a further iota of Bible study, he blurted out: *"My Lord and my God!"*[14]

Do we want another witness? Try the belligerent Saul of Tarsus on the Damascus Road. Lying down there in the dirt, he didn't do a new Bible review course either, but a rapid rebound, *"Who are you, Lord?"*[15] He found out!

Both of these incidents leap from the bedrock of biblical revelation. A divine wake-up call is a fundamental happening all the way across the Good Book from Genesis through Revelation.

I have followed some amazing down-to-earth post-death experiences as one more glitch of erroneous Hellenist assumptions. It can be quite clear, that in crossing the finish line of humanity's big race—aka crossing the Jordan—and throughout the Holy Writ, we have yet to discover any text whatsoever that the game is all over at the last breath. That's from Greek gobbledygook—gobbled up whole by the naïve and passed on to others as gospel truth by the even more naïve!

And that is not to suggest a second chance. It's the finale of the first chance! Life goes on. The spiral goes on. Certainly there is a point of no return, but Scripture does not define it. And anyone eagerly expecting to meet his Messiah won't need his cell phone to find him! But of course there is a final Judgement!

The classic cliché occurring at least 36 times in the Hebrew Scriptures is: *"He rested (or slept) with his fathers,"* and reflects Hebrew faith versus a humanistic formulae. Of course, it may be less than restful if you don't happen to be anticipating your Messiah en route!

And then Yeshua is massively misquoted almost in every step he took across the Galilee by those not on the same page and *fearful of being on* the same page! The key source book of what he really did claim was the Scriptures—particularly the Hebrew prophets.

One other interesting search is whether the ultimate ingathering of Israel is in belief or unbelief—i.e. a sincere anticipation of their coming Messiah or else a total oblivion to what is going on inside the Holy of Holies. If one knows the Scriptures—and the history of human nature—it has to be in unbelief not the perfected fine tuning for paradise one might expect.

For one last time, may we consider the elements of prophesy for that last call for the ingathering of Israel in our former passage of Ezekiel 36:24-28 a few pages back.

First in obvious unbelief, there is a gathering from across the pagan nations; then there is a cleansing from idolatry; and after that there is an anointing by the Ruach.[16] Again this cannot be from human efforts. And only then, there is that divinely motivated obedience to the King of the Universe along with a godly restoration not previously seen.

This is a very significant issue because there are those who would like to deny the validity of Israel's return to—and UN recognition of—their ancient homeland in 1948. Naysayers from Ultra Orthodox to secular, from left wing radicals to right wing zealots and everything in between, protest that in 1948 those sanctified New Jerusalemites posited by the armchair prophets are nowhere to be found—and a political Jerusalem can't be real, they'd like to tell us!

Nevertheless it's been prophesied that redemption will come in a time of primarily unbelief!

In addition to a spot check of the Ezekiel 36 passage above,

here's one more clincher to the question of whether Israel's ultimate return begins in their belief or unbelief. The specific scenario
is detailed in Zechariah 3:1-9.[17]

> *"Then he showed me Joshua the high priest standing before the
> angel of the Lord, and Satan standing at his right side to accuse
> him. The Lord said to Satan, 'The Lord rebuke you, Satan!
> The Lord, who has chosen Jerusalem, rebuke you! Is not this
> man a burning stick snatched from the fire?'*
>
> *"Now Joshua was dressed in filthy clothes as he stood before the
> angel. The angel said to those who were standing before him,
> 'Take off his filthy clothes.' Then he said to Joshua, 'See, I have
> taken away your sin, and I will put fine garments on you.'*
>
> *"Then I said, 'Put a clean turban on his head.' So they put a
> clean turban on his head and clothed him, while the angel of
> the Lord stood by. The angel of the Lord gave this charge to
> Joshua: 'This is what the Lord Almighty says: "If you will walk
> in obedience to me and keep my requirements, then you will
> govern my house and have charge of my courts, and I will give
> you a place among these standing here."*
>
> *"'Listen, High Priest Joshua, you and your associates seated be-
> fore you, who are men symbolic of things to come: I am going to
> bring my servant, the Branch...' says the Lord Almighty, 'and I
> will remove the sin of this land in a single day.'"*

Joshua the High Priest is unquestionably the prophetically returned Israel; and he is ultimately cleansed, forgiven, and reinstated
from his corruption among the nations. The matter is closed:
Latter day Israel initially returns in unbelief!

Sorry Messer's Aristotle, Plato, Pericles, et al, we appreciate
your interest and your input but not your shortcuts! The Good
Book of the Judeo-Christians tells it a bit differently, and we'll
prefer to stick with that.

A possibly under-publicized quote from my earlier book: *Nineveh, a Parody of the Present*,[18] bears repeating: "From the Sanhedrin of the Sages to the Seminaries of the Top Gentile scholars, the Almighty never answers to theology…theology always must answer to God."

Not a bad wake-up call for the whole wobbly world at this point of time!

The bottom line is we are all going to need an ID check on our crossing over into the hereafter, and it probably won't be done by the CIA, the Mossad, the Chief Rabbinate, John Calvin, or even Perry Pericles! That also makes very good sense!

Likewise, no one will ever convince most of us that Annas and Caiaphas had a green light at all intersections, as well as many a Rabbi who may have thought that he himself was Moses reincarnated. Of course that would equally apply to infallibility from popes to plastic professions of faith for time and eternity, including the audacity of allowing Protestant theologian's notes and private interpretations[19] to be printed in the *King James Bible*—or any Bible!

Are we by now aware of the immense anti-Semitic hatred generated through lies and propaganda from the Gaza debacle? Gaza didn't just happen like the so-called Big Bang didn't just happen. Someone had to light the fuse! The reason—the Creator is using anti-Semitism to separate the sheep from the goats.[20] Or more informal word picture from my younger days: Separating the men from the boys in life's battle over the odds.

Like Amalek,[21] there will always be the next battle. In the Gazas of life there will always be the "lawn to mow" again. Retirement is not in the Chosen Service contract. There are always more miles after going the second one.

Putting up with anti-Semitism is an identical concept. It's not going to go away. Conquering it is our channel for a divinely ordered opportunity for change. There is more gold to refine in all of us. No one—Jew or Gentile is finished yet. How many times have we thought about trying to reform old Snake Eyes? It's absurd! Remember he's been in the equation since Genesis 3:15:

> *"God told the serpent: 'Because you've done this, you're cursed, cursed beyond all cattle and wild animals, Cursed to slink on your belly and eat dirt all your life. I'm declaring war between you and the Woman, between your offspring and hers. He'll wound your head, you'll wound his heel.'"* [22]

But we're ready for the next fireworks. Surprises are coming. Bring them on, Abba! Bring them on.

Finally, do me a favor and allow me to have one last poetic shot at anti-Semitism:

The Most High gives the options,
And rebels take the bait.
Humanity is tested
But Truth will compensate.
For Chosenness bears purpose,
Plus a crown to celebrate!

Endnotes

FOREWORD

[1] *Illustrated Sunday Herald,* February 8, 1920, page 5.

[2] "The Final Resolution," p 189, *Jewish World Periodical,* 1908.

[3] Speech to Zionists of America Convention, August 26, 1960.

[4] Israel's first Prime Minister.

[5] German dramatist, novelist and poet (1749-1832).

[6] John Adams, second U.S. president, from a letter to F.A. Van der Kemp (Feb. 16, 1808) Pennsylvania Historical Society.

[7] Op-Ed, *LA Times,* May 26, 1968.

[8] *The National Jewish Post & Observer,* June 6, 1984.

CHAPTER 1

[1] For those interested, her name is Chava in Hebrew.

[2] www.spim.org.au.

[3] Read about the hidden treasure of Stone Age revelation in another day and at another time by *Victor Schlatter, Genetically Modified Prophecies, Whatever Happened to all the Sand and Stars God Promised to Abraham?* (Mobile, AL: Evergreen Press, 2012), chapter 5, p 35.

[4] Genesis 2:19-20.

[5] See Genesis 3:23-24.

[6] These are the current abbreviations of Al-Qaida offshoots from the blood soaked disintegration of a former Syria and Iraq representing: Islamic State, Islamic State in Syria, and Islamic State in Syria and Iraq in Levant.

[7] An interesting aside, as I prepare this manuscript, is that a magnificent view of a little known and less than publicized ancient Valley of Dothan lies directly beyond our front patio.

CHAPTER 2

[1] Tevye—lead character in renowned musical, "Fiddler on the Roof."

[2] For a more complete discussion: Victor Schlatter, *Who Told You that You Were Naked?* (Shippensburg PA, Destiny Image, 2006) See Ch 3: The Mind-Benders Bend Bedrock.

[3] Certainly this did not represent the entire Presbyterian Church, nevertheless the indecency did leave a stain on the remaining more honorable parishioners.

[4] See Joshua 14:1-2 and 5 on the Lord's directive in land division for the twelve tribes.

⁵ Ramah is generally considered to be the birthplace of Prophet Samuel located in Benjamin, approximately twelve miles north of Jerusalem and known as the Arabic administered Ramallah today.

⁶ *Goyim* is the Hebrew expression for Gentiles or the nations.

CHAPTER 3

¹ See Exodus 12:11. Eat it in haste!

² Joshua 5:8 implies not all on the wilderness journey had been circumcised including foreigners but that was changed shortly after crossing the Jordan River.

³ See Chapter 2 "An Expanded Family in a Wider Wilderness," p 14-15.

⁴ Early translations define her as a prostitute, but most likely she was merely an innkeeper and ran the hotel.

⁵ Genesis 12:3. "Whoever blesses you, I will bless!"

⁶ See Hebrews 11:31; James 2:25.

⁷ That is ancient Hebrew.

⁸ A new global voice, pro-Jewish Cyrus King of Persia spearheaded a restoration of Jerusalem, and Nehemiah was given responsibility to oversee rebuilding the wall.

⁹ See Nehemiah 13:3 on a different mix of the multitude; also Chapter 9 or all 13 chapters for those not familiar with the issue.

¹⁰ Genesis 12:6-7.

¹¹ If you are not familiar with the intriguing narrative of Ruth, this would be an excellent time to review it.

¹² Deuteronomy 23:3.

¹³ http://einron.hubpages.com/hub/twosisterstwonationstwoenemies This URL includes Orpah's historical specifics: Orpah differed from her sister Ruth for she returned to Moab where she married a Philistine from the giant race of the Rephaites. Orpah gave birth to Ishbi, the father of Barzillai, the father of Goliath of Gath. Orpah was very unhappy and longed for death because her son was involved in terrorism and murder. She had her chance of belonging to the family who believed in God, but she returned to the land of worshipping idols. Thus God rejected her.

¹⁴ 1 Samuel 17:4-51 (particularly vs. 26 & 41-51).

CHAPTER 4

¹ Torah is the designation for the first five books in the Holy Bible, ascribed to be written down by Moses, and reverenced as such by all God-fearing Jews, Messianic Jews, and Gentiles.

[2] See both Mark 3:4 and Luke 6:9.

[3] "Have you never read what David did when he and his companions were hungry? He entered the house of God, and taking the consecrated bread, he ate what is lawful only for priests to eat. And he also gave some to his companions" (Luke 6:3-4).

[4] Matthew 5:17.

[5] Trypho was an unidentified Jew, a contemporary with Justin Martyr.

[6] Compare "redefiners of righteousness" with Eph. 4:29 "on corrupt communication" (KJV).

[7] Our spelling checker wanted to put another "m" on Grim. Sorry, pun intended!

[8] The most inhuman practice by Hamas TV is idolizing and promoting suicide bombing among children from ages 4 to 10 to the pride of their parents.

[9] Romans 11:28 NKJV.

[10] Jeremiah 31:3.

CHAPTER 5

[1] Genesis 2:17.

[2] On the Maccabees saga see:
https://www.jewishvirtuallibrary.org/jsource/History/Maccabees.html.

[3] Victor Schlatter, on Constantine: *Nineveh, A Parody of the Present: Biblical Clues to the Rise and Fall of America*, Ch 7, (Mobile, AL: Evergreen Press, 2010) p 82.

[4] See: The Maccabees vs. Hellenism.
https://www.jewishvirtuallibrary.org/jsource/History/Maccabees.html.

[5] Genesis 16:11-12.

[6] Victor Schlatter, on Constantine: *Nineveh, A Parody of the Present: Biblical Clues to the Rise and Fall of America*, Ch 7, (Mobile, AL: Evergreen Press, 2010) Heading: Constantine's Crafty Curriculum p 82-84.

[7] See Aldous Huxley, *Brave New World* (Harper & Brothers 1932, USA), which book itself is a cynical forecast of the flow-on of Hellenistic humanism.

[8] http://fromdeathtolife.org/cphil/lsp1.html.

[9] http://internationalpoliticaltheory.blogspot.co.il/2012/03/political-thought-of-st-augustine.html.

[10] For more complete insight on the gulf between Greek and Hebraic mindset see: Victor Schlatter, *Who Told You that You Were Naked?*

(Shippensburg PA, Destiny Image, 2006), Ch 3: The Mind-Benders bend Bedrock.

[11] www.biography.com/people/st-thomas-aquinas-9187231#early-life.

[12] Translated by Martin H. Bertram, *On The Jews and Their Lies, Luther's Works, Volume 47*; Philadelphia: Fortress Press, 1971.

[13] http://kenanmalik.wordpress.com/2011/10/14/a-book-in-progress-part-9-martin-luthers-accidental-revolution/.

[14] Jeremiah 2:11 NKJV.

[15] Excerpt from "Ad Quaelstiones et Objecta Juaei Cuiusdam Responsio," by John Calvin; *The Jew in Christian Theology*, Gerhard Falk (McFarland and Company, Inc., Jefferson, NC and London, 1931).

[16] http://www.iep.utm.edu/calvin/.

CHAPTER 6

[1] Two translations utilize "first." *The Message Bible* has:"First this: God created the heavens and the earth." *The Living Bible* catches the Hebraic sense even better: "When God began creating the heavens and the earth..."

[2] There are some 16 references, Exodus to Deuteronomy for Rock or rock that is a direct reference to the Angel of God (Ex 14:19) both seen and unseen, preceding or following the Israelites from Egypt to the Jordan.

[3] In Hebrew the word for messenger and angel are the same and differentiated in translation by context.

[4] That is, the Righteous King in Hebrew, presumed by many scholars as a divine pre-appearance of Messiah.

[5] The climate has changed dramatically since the Ice Age but by whom and why?

[6] For more details of the Avram Pamu discovery, including 4 of the 10 Commandments, see Victor Schlatter, *Genetically Modified Prophecies*, (Mobile, AL: Evergreen Press, 2012) Chapter 6, Who Was Avram Pamu, p 40.

[7] /b/ and /v/ are interchangeable in most Hebrew contexts.

[8] Genesis 17:3-8.

[9] Tevye—lead character in renowned musical, *Fiddler on the Roof*.

[10] Exodus Chapter 2:1-4.

[11] Of a multitude of phenomena attributed to Moses' involvement, one of the most significant indications of credibility was the discovery of ancient Egyptian chariot wheels on the floor of the Red Sea much in the re-searched path of the Exodus.

[12] See 1 Kings 19:9-18 and surrounding scenario for the "gentle whisper" aka "still small voice."

CHAPTER 7

[1] An Australian slang expression meaning to "go native."

[2] *Yegi* is simply a Waola name. *Isi hobao sao* ironically means the "important son" in a culture totally devoid of any New Testament era contact.

[3] This novel assumption was also related in a lecture by Prime Minister Sitiveni Rabuka of Fiji in 1994.

[4] The *mumu* is a traditional Pacific Island cooking with hot rocks and banana-leaf lining in a shallow pit.

[5] September 2014.

[6] See Ch 6. BBII is the tongue-in-cheek acronym for Burning Bush Information Institute in a parody of Ex 3:1-4.

[7] Across Scripture two or three witnesses are required for accuracy in decisions: e.g. Deut. 19:15; Mt. 18:16; 1 Tim. 5:19.

[8] Hebrew for Holy Spirit.

[9] As Endnote 5 above, BBII is a tongue-in-cheek acronym for Burning Bush Institute of Information.

[10] Job 23:10.

[11] 1 Cor. 2:9; Isaiah 64:4.

CHAPTER 8

[1] Exodus 17:16: He said, *"Because hands were lifted up against the throne of the LORD, the LORD will be at war against the Amalekites from generation to generation."*

[2] Victor Schlatter, *Nineveh, A Parody of the Present: Biblical Clues to the Rise and Fall of America* (Mobile, AL: Evergreen Press, 2010).

[3] The average age of political might of nations across biblical tenure is around 200 years, except for Israel and Egypt, both of which still remain as a national entity.

[4] On conquering Jerusalem in 132 AD, Roman Emperor Hadrian renamed the land Falestina in bias of the Jews' arch-rival, the Philistines, inflicting added grief to the loss of their treasured homeland.

[5] Egyptian Arafat was certainly not what would have been known as a Palestinian.

[6] The acronym for: Middle East Media and Research Institute.

[7] The acronym for: Committee for Accuracy in Middle East Reporting in America.

[8] Jeremiah 31:35-37.

[9] More promises for Israel's return and restoration include: Isa. 43:5-6; Jer. 23:7-8; Joel 3: 20; Amos 9:14-15.

[10] *New Living Testament.*

[11] The para-message in protracted Psalm 119 is the usage of five terms with parallel meaning that override a more mundane text with the exultancy of God, God, God.

CHAPTER 9

[1] The game is hardly new. See Genesis 3:5.

[2] See Matthew 16:13-18.

[3] Australian terminology for rugby.

[4] Plural of sarcophagus.

[5] For the infamous event of the Golden Calf, see Exodus 32:15-24.

[6] 2 Cor 11:22-28 (edited portions).

[7] For a generation that has missed out, Silver was the name of the Lone Ranger's horse and makes a fitting finale for considering individualism.

[8] 2 Timothy 4:7.

[9] Some of the greatest anti-Semites of our day are influential Jewish journalists and financiers who fund Islamic terror organizations endeavoring to undermine the Jewish State.

[10] See Exodus 17:14-15 and Deuteronomy 25:17-19.

CHAPTER 10

[1] April 2013.

[2] Spirit, i.e. the Holy Spirit.

[3] See Isaiah 6:3-8.

[4] The Gentiles or the Nations.

[5] See Matthew 24:21 and Daniel 12:1.

[6] The setting is reminiscent of despot Joseph Stalin's use of "useful idiots" in reference to his proletariat.

[7] See Genesis 3:14-15.

[8] See Genesis 22:1-18.

[9] *Ketuvim* is the name in the Hebrew Tanach for the "writings"—the Psalms, Proverbs, Job and others.

CHAPTER 11

[1] Adapted from Kate Smith's classic quip of Grand Ole Opry days in the 1950s, originally: "Fat Lady" sings.

2 References: Matthew 24:13; Mark 13:13.

3 John 16:33.

4 Revelations 2:5.

5 Revelations 3:10.

6 Job 13:15.

7 It is presumed that the Hebrew prophet Isaiah was the one referred to above who was slashed in two.

8 The spelling is correct, and the pun very much intended!

9 Isaiah 60:19-20. See also: Rev 22:5, Rev 21:23 & Isaiah 24:23.

10 Genesis 14:18-20.

11 Including 1 Cor. 10:4.

12 Compare with Daniel 7:25.

13 John 20:25.

14 John 20:28.

15 Acts 9:5.

16 The Holy Spirit.

17 Slightly truncated for continuity of the them.

18 Victor Schlatter, *Nineveh, A Parody of the Present: Biblical Clues to the Rise and Fall of America* (Mobile, AL : Evergreen Press, 2010) .

19 2 Peter 1:20 NKJV.

20 See Matthew 25:31-46.

21 Exodus 17:16.

22 From *The Message* Bible.

OTHER BOOKS BY VICTOR SCHLATTER

Where is the Body? Discovering the Church in the Heart of Israel
is a wake-up call in these dire days of Israel's restoration and testing, to jar the church into an awakening to God's unique plan of a reborn Israel in an advent of a Messianic Age. It exposes not a few faulty end-time fables that via anti-Semitic bias have feigned honesty in much of the Church. Its aim is reality, truth and above all, faithfully cites the Bible you say you believe.

Showdown of the Gods: The Global Confrontation Between Islam, Humanism, and God
ironically went to press on 9-11, 2001, *Showdown* links ancient Bible prophets to a morally and spiritually decaying globe. It sees daily disasters around us in the light of prophecy, exposing unlikely bedfellows—Islam and New World Order humanism. Both vying for a final crack at a Creator God—at first to feign friendship, finally to draw blood—the nightly news won't surprise old Zechariah!

Who Told You, You Were Naked? From the Fall of Adam to the Rise of the Antichrist
uncovers the naked truth of an unbridgeable chasm between eastern Hebraic and western Greek thinking. You will gain amazing new insight into Media Bias, Humanism, Organized Religion, Political Correctness, and a God-defying New World Order.

Nineveh: A Parody of the Present, Biblical Clues on the Rise and Fall of America
is an overview of waning days as a superpower, by biblically viewing her aside the deeds and demise of 5 ancient kingdoms that have long since descended those trails of no return—Nineveh, Babylon, Persia, Greece and Rome and now post Roman Europe. It's anything but heavy laden history, laced with quips and prickly truth that the Western World must learn.

Genetically Modified Prophecies
Discover what happened to the promise that God made to Abraham about his descendants being innumerable. Gives new ideas from a research scholar and Wycliffe translator. Proof abounds in plain sight that God was right all along!

Author contact information:
website: http://www.spim.org.au

General book availability:
spimaust@gmail.com, www.Amazon.com, spimusa@gmail.com

Contacts in Australia:
adminaust@bridgesforpeace.com.au

Contacts in Israel:
www.galileeexperience.com, Emmanuel Bookshop-Jaffa Gate or Galilee Experience-Tiberias, and Bible Bookshops worldwide.

More on SPIM, Inc. (South Pacific Island Ministries) is posted on:
http://www.spim.org.au

About the Author

VICTOR SCHLATTER spent seven years as a nuclear scientist before heeding a higher call to upgrade his scientific career to Linguistic Analysis and Bible translation. In a South Pacific Stone Age scenario, he translated the Waola Scriptures now in their fifth printing. He found that there is no such thing as a primitive language, since Stone Age Waola has over 100 endings on every verb! His translation has since generated over 130 tribal congregations with some 15,000 believers across Papua New Guinea.

The Schlatters then reached out in a Pacific-wide ministry linking Isaiah's oft repeated "Islands of the Sea" to a long-prophesied Israel reborn. Having made annual trips to Jerusalem since 1988, he has maintained in-depth research on the ever-escalating, never-ending Middle East countdown, especially as it reflects biblical prophecy. He is founder and Director of South Pacific Island Ministries, represents the International Christian Embassy Jerusalem to the South Pacific Islands, and lectures globally.

He was awarded the Queen's Papua New Guinea Independence Medal in 1975 for recognized service to the Southern Highlands, and was selected for Who's Who in Queensland, Australia, in 2007. He is the author of *Where Is the Body?* (translated into Russian, Finnish, and Dutch); *Showdown of the Gods; Who Told You that You Were Naked?; Nineveh: A Parody of the Present—Biblical Clues to the Rise and Fall of America;* and *Genetically Modified Prophecies— Whatever Happened to all the Sand and Stars God Promised to Abraham?*

He and his wife, Elsie, reside in Australia.